William Shakespeare (bapt. 26 April 1564 – 23 April 1616) was an English poet, playwright and actor, widely regarded as the greatest writer in the English language and the world's greatest dramatist. He is often called England's national poet and the "Bard of Avon". His extant works, including collaborations, consist of approximately 39 plays, 154 sonnets, two long narrative poems, and a few other verses, some of uncertain authorship. His plays have been translated into every major living language and are performed more often than those of any other playwright. Shakespeare was born and raised in Stratford-upon-Avon, Warwickshire. At the age of 18, he married Anne Hathaway, with whom he had three children: Susanna and twins Hamnet and Judith. Sometime between 1585 and 1592, he began a successful career in London as an actor, writer, and part-owner of a playing company called the Lord Chamberlain's Men, later known as the King's Men. At age 49 (around 1613), he appears to have retired to Stratford, where he died three years later. (Source: Wikipedia)

Literary works:
The Tempest
The Two Gentlemen of Verona
The Merry Wives of Windsor
Measure for Measure
The Comedy of Errors
Much Ado About Nothing
Love's Labour's Lost
A Midsummer Night's Dream
The Merchant of Venice
As You Like It
The Taming of the Shrew
All's Well That Ends Well
Twelfth Night
The Winter's Tale
Pericles, Prince of Tyre
The Two Noble Kinsmen

JULIUS CAESAR

William Shakespeare

PRINCE CLASSICS

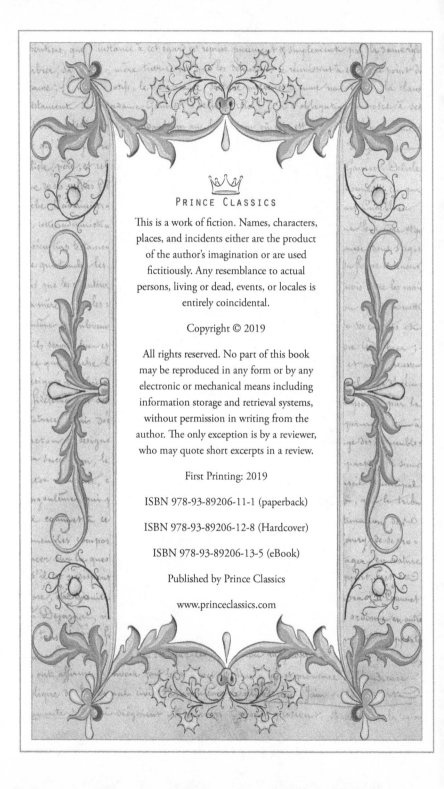

PRINCE CLASSICS

First Printing: 2019

ISBN 978-93-89206-11-1 (paperback)

ISBN 978-93-89206-12-8 (Hardcover)

ISBN 978-93-89206-13-5 (eBook)

Published by Prince Classics

www.princeclassics.com

Contents

JULIUS CAESAR

Dramatis Personæ

JULIUS CAESAR

OCTAVIUS CAESAR, Triumvir after his death.

MARCUS ANTONIUS, " " "

M. AEMILIUS LEPIDUS, " " "

CICERO, PUBLIUS, POPILIUS LENA, Senators.

MARCUS BRUTUS, Conspirator against Caesar.

CASSIUS, " " "

CASCA, " " "

TREBONIUS, " " "

LIGARIUS," " "

DECIUS BRUTUS, " " "

METELLUS CIMBER, " " "

CINNA, " " "

FLAVIUS, tribune

MARULLUS, tribune

ARTEMIDORUS, a Sophist of Cnidos.

A Soothsayer

CINNA, a poet.

Another Poet.

LUCILIUS, TITINIUS, MESSALA, young CATO, and VOLUMNIUS, Friends to Brutus and Cassius.

VARRO, CLITUS, CLAUDIUS, STRATO, LUCIUS, DARDANIUS, Servants to Brutus

PINDARUS, Servant to Cassius

CALPHURNIA, wife to Caesar

PORTIA, wife to Brutus

The Ghost of Caesar

Senators, Citizens, Soldiers, Commoners, Messengers, and Servants.

SCENE: Rome, the conspirators' camp near Sardis, and the plains of Philippi.

ACT I

SCENE I. Rome. A street.

Enter Flavius, Marullus and a throng of Citizens.

FLAVIUS.

Hence! home, you idle creatures, get you home.

Is this a holiday? What, know you not,

Being mechanical, you ought not walk

Upon a labouring day without the sign

Of your profession? Speak, what trade art thou?

CARPENTER.

Why, sir, a carpenter.

MARULLUS.

Where is thy leather apron and thy rule?

What dost thou with thy best apparel on?

You, sir, what trade are you?

COBBLER.

Truly, sir, in respect of a fine workman, I am but, as you would say, a cobbler.

MARULLUS.

But what trade art thou? Answer me directly.

COBBLER.

A trade, sir, that I hope I may use with a safe conscience, which is indeed, sir, a mender of bad soles.

MARULLUS.

What trade, thou knave? Thou naughty knave, what trade?

COBBLER.

Nay, I beseech you, sir, be not out with me; yet, if you be out, sir, I can mend you.

MARULLUS.

What mean'st thou by that? Mend me, thou saucy fellow!

COBBLER.

Why, sir, cobble you.

FLAVIUS.

Thou art a cobbler, art thou?

COBBLER.

Truly, sir, all that I live by is with the awl; I meddle with no tradesman's matters, nor women's matters, but withal I am indeed, sir, a surgeon to old shoes: when they are in great danger, I recover them. As proper men as ever trod upon neat's leather have gone upon my handiwork.

FLAVIUS.

But wherefore art not in thy shop today?

Why dost thou lead these men about the streets?

COBBLER.

Truly, sir, to wear out their shoes, to get myself into more work. But indeed, sir, we make holiday to see Caesar, and to rejoice in his triumph.

MARULLUS.

Wherefore rejoice? What conquest brings he home?

What tributaries follow him to Rome,

To grace in captive bonds his chariot wheels?

You blocks, you stones, you worse than senseless things!

O you hard hearts, you cruel men of Rome,

Knew you not Pompey? Many a time and oft

Have you climb'd up to walls and battlements,

To towers and windows, yea, to chimney tops,

Your infants in your arms, and there have sat

The livelong day with patient expectation,

To see great Pompey pass the streets of Rome.

And when you saw his chariot but appear,

Have you not made an universal shout,

That Tiber trembled underneath her banks

To hear the replication of your sounds

Made in her concave shores?

And do you now put on your best attire?

And do you now cull out a holiday?

And do you now strew flowers in his way,

That comes in triumph over Pompey's blood?

Be gone!

Run to your houses, fall upon your knees,

Pray to the gods to intermit the plague

That needs must light on this ingratitude.

FLAVIUS.

Go, go, good countrymen, and, for this fault

Assemble all the poor men of your sort,

Draw them to Tiber banks, and weep your tears

Into the channel, till the lowest stream

Do kiss the most exalted shores of all.

[Exeunt Citizens.]

See whether their basest metal be not mov'd;

They vanish tongue-tied in their guiltiness.

Go you down that way towards the Capitol;

This way will I. Disrobe the images,

If you do find them deck'd with ceremonies.

MARULLUS.

May we do so?

You know it is the feast of Lupercal.

FLAVIUS.

It is no matter; let no images

Be hung with Caesar's trophies. I'll about

And drive away the vulgar from the streets;

So do you too, where you perceive them thick.

These growing feathers pluck'd from Caesar's wing

Will make him fly an ordinary pitch,

Who else would soar above the view of men,

And keep us all in servile fearfulness.

[Exeunt.]

SCENE II. The same. A public place.

Enter, in procession, with music, Caesar; Antony, for the course; Calphurnia, Portia, Decius, Cicero, Brutus, Cassius and Casca; a great crowd following, among them a Soothsayer.

CAESAR.

Calphurnia.

CASCA.

Peace, ho! Caesar speaks.

[Music ceases.]

CAESAR.

Calphurnia.

CALPHURNIA.

Here, my lord.

CAESAR.

Stand you directly in Antonius' way,

When he doth run his course. Antonius.

ANTONY.

Caesar, my lord?

CAESAR.

Forget not in your speed, Antonius,

To touch Calphurnia; for our elders say,

The barren, touched in this holy chase,

Shake off their sterile curse.

ANTONY.

I shall remember.

When Caesar says "Do this," it is perform'd.

CAESAR.

Set on; and leave no ceremony out.

[Music.]

SOOTHSAYER.

Caesar!

CAESAR.

Ha! Who calls?

CASCA.

Bid every noise be still; peace yet again!

[Music ceases.]

CAESAR.

Who is it in the press that calls on me?

I hear a tongue shriller than all the music,

Cry "Caesar"! Speak. Caesar is turn'd to hear.

SOOTHSAYER.

Beware the Ides of March.

CAESAR.

What man is that?

BRUTUS.

A soothsayer bids you beware the Ides of March.

CAESAR.

Set him before me; let me see his face.

CASSIUS.

Fellow, come from the throng; look upon Caesar.

CAESAR.

What say'st thou to me now? Speak once again.

SOOTHSAYER.

Beware the Ides of March.

CAESAR.

He is a dreamer; let us leave him. Pass.

[Sennet. Exeunt all but Brutus and Cassius.]

CASSIUS.

Will you go see the order of the course?

BRUTUS.

Not I.

CASSIUS.

I pray you, do.

BRUTUS.

I am not gamesome: I do lack some part

Of that quick spirit that is in Antony.

Let me not hinder, Cassius, your desires;

I'll leave you.

CASSIUS.

Brutus, I do observe you now of late:

I have not from your eyes that gentleness

And show of love as I was wont to have.

You bear too stubborn and too strange a hand

Over your friend that loves you.

BRUTUS.

Cassius,

Be not deceived: if I have veil'd my look,

I turn the trouble of my countenance

Merely upon myself. Vexed I am

Of late with passions of some difference,

Conceptions only proper to myself,

Which give some soil perhaps to my behaviors;

But let not therefore my good friends be grieved

(Among which number, Cassius, be you one)

Nor construe any further my neglect,

Than that poor Brutus, with himself at war,

Forgets the shows of love to other men.

CASSIUS.

Then, Brutus, I have much mistook your passion;

By means whereof this breast of mine hath buried

Thoughts of great value, worthy cogitations.

Tell me, good Brutus, can you see your face?

BRUTUS.

No, Cassius, for the eye sees not itself

But by reflection, by some other thing.

CASSIUS.

'Tis just:

And it is very much lamented, Brutus,

That you have no such mirrors as will turn

Your hidden worthiness into your eye,

That you might see your shadow. I have heard

Where many of the best respect in Rome,

(Except immortal Caesar) speaking of Brutus,

And groaning underneath this age's yoke,

Have wish'd that noble Brutus had his eyes.

BRUTUS.

Into what dangers would you lead me, Cassius,

That you would have me seek into myself

For that which is not in me?

CASSIUS.

Therefore, good Brutus, be prepared to hear;

And since you know you cannot see yourself

So well as by reflection, I, your glass,

Will modestly discover to yourself

That of yourself which you yet know not of.

And be not jealous on me, gentle Brutus:

Were I a common laugher, or did use

To stale with ordinary oaths my love

To every new protester; if you know

That I do fawn on men, and hug them hard,

And after scandal them; or if you know

That I profess myself in banqueting,

To all the rout, then hold me dangerous.

[Flourish and shout.]

BRUTUS.

What means this shouting? I do fear the people

Choose Caesar for their king.

CASSIUS.

Ay, do you fear it?

Then must I think you would not have it so.

BRUTUS.

I would not, Cassius; yet I love him well,

But wherefore do you hold me here so long?

What is it that you would impart to me?

If it be aught toward the general good,

Set honour in one eye and death i' the other,

And I will look on both indifferently;

For let the gods so speed me as I love

The name of honour more than I fear death.

CASSIUS.

I know that virtue to be in you, Brutus,

As well as I do know your outward favour.

Well, honour is the subject of my story.

I cannot tell what you and other men

Think of this life; but, for my single self,

I had as lief not be as live to be

In awe of such a thing as I myself.

I was born free as Caesar; so were you;

We both have fed as well, and we can both

Endure the winter's cold as well as he:

For once, upon a raw and gusty day,

The troubled Tiber chafing with her shores,

Caesar said to me, "Dar'st thou, Cassius, now

Leap in with me into this angry flood,

And swim to yonder point?" Upon the word,

Accoutred as I was, I plunged in,

And bade him follow: so indeed he did.

The torrent roar'd, and we did buffet it

With lusty sinews, throwing it aside

And stemming it with hearts of controversy.

But ere we could arrive the point propos'd,

Caesar cried, "Help me, Cassius, or I sink!"

I, as Aeneas, our great ancestor,

Did from the flames of Troy upon his shoulder

The old Anchises bear, so from the waves of Tiber

Did I the tired Caesar. And this man

Is now become a god; and Cassius is

A wretched creature, and must bend his body,

If Caesar carelessly but nod on him.

He had a fever when he was in Spain,

And when the fit was on him I did mark

How he did shake: 'tis true, this god did shake:

His coward lips did from their colour fly,

And that same eye whose bend doth awe the world

Did lose his lustre. I did hear him groan:

Ay, and that tongue of his, that bade the Romans

Mark him, and write his speeches in their books,

Alas, it cried, "Give me some drink, Titinius,"

As a sick girl. Ye gods, it doth amaze me,

A man of such a feeble temper should

So get the start of the majestic world,

And bear the palm alone.

[Shout. Flourish.]

BRUTUS.

Another general shout?

I do believe that these applauses are

For some new honours that are heap'd on Caesar.

CASSIUS.

Why, man, he doth bestride the narrow world

Like a Colossus, and we petty men

Walk under his huge legs, and peep about

To find ourselves dishonourable graves.

Men at some time are masters of their fates:

The fault, dear Brutus, is not in our stars,

But in ourselves, that we are underlings.

"Brutus" and "Caesar": what should be in that "Caesar"?

Why should that name be sounded more than yours?

Write them together, yours is as fair a name;

Sound them, it doth become the mouth as well;

Weigh them, it is as heavy; conjure with 'em,

"Brutus" will start a spirit as soon as "Caesar."

Now in the names of all the gods at once,

Upon what meat doth this our Caesar feed,

That he is grown so great? Age, thou art sham'd!

Rome, thou hast lost the breed of noble bloods!

When went there by an age since the great flood,

But it was fam'd with more than with one man?

When could they say, till now, that talk'd of Rome,

That her wide walls encompass'd but one man?

Now is it Rome indeed, and room enough,

When there is in it but one only man.

O, you and I have heard our fathers say,

There was a Brutus once that would have brook'd

Th' eternal devil to keep his state in Rome,

As easily as a king!

BRUTUS.

That you do love me, I am nothing jealous;

What you would work me to, I have some aim:

How I have thought of this, and of these times,

I shall recount hereafter. For this present,

I would not, so with love I might entreat you,

Be any further mov'd. What you have said,

I will consider; what you have to say

I will with patience hear; and find a time

Both meet to hear and answer such high things.

Till then, my noble friend, chew upon this:

Brutus had rather be a villager

Than to repute himself a son of Rome

Under these hard conditions as this time

Is like to lay upon us.

CASSIUS.

I am glad that my weak words

Have struck but thus much show of fire from Brutus.

Enter Caesar and his Train.

BRUTUS.

The games are done, and Caesar is returning.

CASSIUS.

As they pass by, pluck Casca by the sleeve,

And he will, after his sour fashion, tell you

What hath proceeded worthy note today.

BRUTUS.

I will do so. But, look you, Cassius,

The angry spot doth glow on Caesar's brow,

And all the rest look like a chidden train:

Calphurnia's cheek is pale; and Cicero

Looks with such ferret and such fiery eyes

As we have seen him in the Capitol,

Being cross'd in conference by some senators.

CASSIUS.

Casca will tell us what the matter is.

CAESAR.

Antonius.

ANTONY.

Caesar?

CAESAR.

Let me have men about me that are fat,

Sleek-headed men, and such as sleep a-nights:

Yond Cassius has a lean and hungry look;

He thinks too much: such men are dangerous.

ANTONY.

Fear him not, Caesar; he's not dangerous;

He is a noble Roman and well given.

CAESAR.

Would he were fatter! But I fear him not:

Yet if my name were liable to fear,

I do not know the man I should avoid

So soon as that spare Cassius. He reads much,

He is a great observer, and he looks

Quite through the deeds of men. He loves no plays,

As thou dost, Antony; he hears no music.

Seldom he smiles; and smiles in such a sort

As if he mock'd himself and scorn'd his spirit

That could be mov'd to smile at anything.

Such men as he be never at heart's ease

Whiles they behold a greater than themselves,

And therefore are they very dangerous.

I rather tell thee what is to be fear'd

Than what I fear; for always I am Caesar.

Come on my right hand, for this ear is deaf,

And tell me truly what thou think'st of him.

[Exeunt Caesar and his Train. Casca stays.]

CASCA.

You pull'd me by the cloak; would you speak with me?

BRUTUS.

Ay, Casca, tell us what hath chanc'd today,

That Caesar looks so sad.

CASCA.

Why, you were with him, were you not?

BRUTUS.

I should not then ask Casca what had chanc'd.

CASCA.

Why, there was a crown offer'd him; and being offer'd him, he put it by with the back of his hand, thus; and then the people fell a-shouting.

BRUTUS.

What was the second noise for?

CASCA.

Why, for that too.

CASSIUS.

They shouted thrice: what was the last cry for?

CASCA.

Why, for that too.

BRUTUS.

Was the crown offer'd him thrice?

CASCA.

Ay, marry, was't, and he put it by thrice, every time gentler than other; and at every putting-by mine honest neighbours shouted.

CASSIUS.

Who offer'd him the crown?

CASCA.

Why, Antony.

BRUTUS.

Tell us the manner of it, gentle Casca.

CASCA.

I can as well be hang'd, as tell the manner of it: it was mere foolery; I did not mark it. I saw Mark Antony offer him a crown; yet 'twas not a crown neither, 'twas one of these coronets; and, as I told you, he put it by once: but, for all that, to my thinking, he would fain have had it. Then he offered it to him again: then he put it by again: but, to my thinking, he was very loath to lay his fingers off it. And then he offered it the third time; he put it the third time by; and still, as he refus'd it, the rabblement hooted, and clapp'd their chopt hands, and threw up their sweaty night-caps, and uttered such a deal of stinking breath because Caesar refus'd the crown, that it had, almost, choked Caesar, for he swooned, and fell down at it. And for mine own part, I durst not laugh, for fear of opening my lips and receiving the bad air.

CASSIUS.

But, soft! I pray you. What, did Caesar swoon?

CASCA.

He fell down in the market-place, and foam'd at mouth, and was speechless.

BRUTUS.

'Tis very like: he hath the falling-sickness.

CASSIUS.

No, Caesar hath it not; but you, and I,

And honest Casca, we have the falling-sickness.

CASCA.

I know not what you mean by that; but I am sure Caesar fell down. If the tag-rag people did not clap him and hiss him, according as he pleased and displeased them, as they use to do the players in the theatre, I am no true man.

BRUTUS.

What said he when he came unto himself?

CASCA.

Marry, before he fell down, when he perceived the common herd was glad he refused the crown, he pluck'd me ope his doublet, and offer'd them his throat to cut. And I had been a man of any occupation, if I would not have taken him at a word, I would I might go to hell among the rogues. And so he fell. When he came to himself again, he said, if he had done or said anything amiss, he desir'd their worships to think it was his infirmity. Three or four wenches where I stood cried, "Alas, good soul!" and forgave him with all their hearts. But there's no heed to be taken of them: if Caesar had stabb'd their mothers, they would have done no less.

BRUTUS.

And, after that, he came thus sad away?

CASCA.

Ay.

CASSIUS.

Did Cicero say anything?

CASCA.

Ay, he spoke Greek.

CASSIUS.

To what effect?

CASCA.

Nay, and I tell you that, I'll ne'er look you i' the face again. But those that understood him smil'd at one another and shook their heads; but for mine own part, it was Greek to me. I could tell you more news too: Marullus and Flavius, for pulling scarfs off Caesar's images, are put to silence. Fare you well. There was more foolery yet, if I could remember it.

CASSIUS.

Will you sup with me tonight, Casca?

CASCA.

No, I am promis'd forth.

CASSIUS.

Will you dine with me tomorrow?

CASCA.

Ay, if I be alive, and your mind hold, and your dinner worth the eating.

CASSIUS.

Good. I will expect you.

CASCA.

Do so; farewell both.

[Exit Casca.]

BRUTUS.

What a blunt fellow is this grown to be!

He was quick mettle when he went to school.

CASSIUS.

So is he now in execution

Of any bold or noble enterprise,

However he puts on this tardy form.

This rudeness is a sauce to his good wit,

Which gives men stomach to digest his words

With better appetite.

BRUTUS.

And so it is. For this time I will leave you:

Tomorrow, if you please to speak with me,

I will come home to you; or, if you will,

Come home to me, and I will wait for you.

CASSIUS.

I will do so: till then, think of the world.

[Exit Brutus.]

Well, Brutus, thou art noble; yet I see,

Thy honourable metal may be wrought

From that it is dispos'd: therefore 'tis meet

That noble minds keep ever with their likes;

For who so firm that cannot be seduc'd?

Caesar doth bear me hard, but he loves Brutus.

If I were Brutus now, and he were Cassius,

He should not humour me. I will this night,

In several hands, in at his windows throw,

As if they came from several citizens,

Writings, all tending to the great opinion

That Rome holds of his name; wherein obscurely

Caesar's ambition shall be glanced at.

And after this, let Caesar seat him sure,

For we will shake him, or worse days endure.

[Exit.]

SCENE III. The same. A street.

Thunder and lightning. Enter, from opposite sides, Casca with his sword drawn, and Cicero.

CICERO.

Good even, Casca: brought you Caesar home?

Why are you breathless, and why stare you so?

CASCA.

Are not you moved, when all the sway of earth

Shakes like a thing unfirm? O Cicero,

I have seen tempests, when the scolding winds

Have riv'd the knotty oaks; and I have seen

Th' ambitious ocean swell and rage and foam,

To be exalted with the threatening clouds:

But never till tonight, never till now,

Did I go through a tempest dropping fire.

Either there is a civil strife in heaven,

Or else the world too saucy with the gods,

Incenses them to send destruction.

CICERO.

Why, saw you anything more wonderful?

CASCA.

A common slave, you'd know him well by sight,

Held up his left hand, which did flame and burn

Like twenty torches join'd, and yet his hand,

Not sensible of fire remain'd unscorch'd.

Besides, I ha' not since put up my sword,

Against the Capitol I met a lion,

Who glared upon me, and went surly by,

Without annoying me. And there were drawn

Upon a heap a hundred ghastly women,

Transformed with their fear; who swore they saw

Men, all in fire, walk up and down the streets.

And yesterday the bird of night did sit,

Even at noonday upon the marketplace,

Hooting and shrieking. When these prodigies

Do so conjointly meet, let not men say,

"These are their reasons; they are natural";

For I believe, they are portentous things

Unto the climate that they point upon.

CICERO.

Indeed, it is a strange-disposed time.

But men may construe things after their fashion,

Clean from the purpose of the things themselves.

Comes Caesar to the Capitol tomorrow?

CASCA.

He doth, for he did bid Antonius

Send word to you he would be there tomorrow.

CICERO.

Goodnight then, Casca: this disturbed sky

Is not to walk in.

CASCA.

Farewell, Cicero.

[Exit Cicero.]

Enter Cassius.

CASSIUS.

Who's there?

CASCA.

A Roman.

CASSIUS.

Casca, by your voice.

CASCA.

Your ear is good. Cassius, what night is this!

CASSIUS.

A very pleasing night to honest men.

CASCA.

Who ever knew the heavens menace so?

CASSIUS.

Those that have known the earth so full of faults.

For my part, I have walk'd about the streets,

Submitting me unto the perilous night;

And, thus unbraced, Casca, as you see,

Have bar'd my bosom to the thunder-stone;

And when the cross blue lightning seem'd to open

The breast of heaven, I did present myself

Even in the aim and very flash of it.

CASCA.

But wherefore did you so much tempt the Heavens?

It is the part of men to fear and tremble,

When the most mighty gods by tokens send

Such dreadful heralds to astonish us.

CASSIUS.

You are dull, Casca; and those sparks of life

That should be in a Roman you do want,

Or else you use not. You look pale and gaze,

And put on fear and cast yourself in wonder,

To see the strange impatience of the Heavens:

But if you would consider the true cause

Why all these fires, why all these gliding ghosts,

Why birds and beasts, from quality and kind;

Why old men, fools, and children calculate,

Why all these things change from their ordinance,

Their natures, and pre-formed faculties,

To monstrous quality; why, you shall find

That Heaven hath infus'd them with these spirits,

To make them instruments of fear and warning

Unto some monstrous state.

Now could I, Casca, name to thee a man

Most like this dreadful night,

That thunders, lightens, opens graves, and roars,

As doth the lion in the Capitol;

A man no mightier than thyself, or me,

In personal action; yet prodigious grown,

And fearful, as these strange eruptions are.

CASCA.

'Tis Caesar that you mean; is it not, Cassius?

CASSIUS.

Let it be who it is: for Romans now

Have thews and limbs like to their ancestors;

But, woe the while! our fathers' minds are dead,

And we are govern'd with our mothers' spirits;

Our yoke and sufferance show us womanish.

CASCA.

Indeed, they say the senators tomorrow

Mean to establish Caesar as a king;

And he shall wear his crown by sea and land,

In every place, save here in Italy.

CASSIUS.

I know where I will wear this dagger then;

Cassius from bondage will deliver Cassius:

Therein, ye gods, you make the weak most strong;

Therein, ye gods, you tyrants do defeat.

Nor stony tower, nor walls of beaten brass,

Nor airless dungeon, nor strong links of iron,

Can be retentive to the strength of spirit;

But life, being weary of these worldly bars,

Never lacks power to dismiss itself.

If I know this, know all the world besides,

That part of tyranny that I do bear

I can shake off at pleasure.

[Thunder still.]

CASCA.

So can I:

So every bondman in his own hand bears

The power to cancel his captivity.

CASSIUS.

And why should Caesar be a tyrant then?

Poor man! I know he would not be a wolf,

But that he sees the Romans are but sheep:

He were no lion, were not Romans hinds.

Those that with haste will make a mighty fire

Begin it with weak straws. What trash is Rome,

What rubbish, and what offal, when it serves

For the base matter to illuminate

So vile a thing as Caesar! But, O grief,

Where hast thou led me? I, perhaps, speak this

Before a willing bondman: then I know

My answer must be made; but I am arm'd,

And dangers are to me indifferent.

CASCA.

You speak to Casca, and to such a man

That is no fleering tell-tale. Hold, my hand:

Be factious for redress of all these griefs,

And I will set this foot of mine as far

As who goes farthest.

CASSIUS.

There's a bargain made.

Now know you, Casca, I have mov'd already

Some certain of the noblest-minded Romans

To undergo with me an enterprise

Of honourable-dangerous consequence;

And I do know by this, they stay for me

In Pompey's Porch: for now, this fearful night,

There is no stir or walking in the streets;

And the complexion of the element

In favour's like the work we have in hand,

Most bloody, fiery, and most terrible.

Enter Cinna.

CASCA.

Stand close awhile, for here comes one in haste.

CASSIUS.

'Tis Cinna; I do know him by his gait;

He is a friend. Cinna, where haste you so?

CINNA.

To find out you. Who's that? Metellus Cimber?

CASSIUS.

No, it is Casca, one incorporate

To our attempts. Am I not stay'd for, Cinna?

CINNA.

I am glad on't. What a fearful night is this!

There's two or three of us have seen strange sights.

CASSIUS.

Am I not stay'd for? tell me.

CINNA.

Yes, you are. O Cassius, if you could

But win the noble Brutus to our party—

CASSIUS.

Be you content. Good Cinna, take this paper,

And look you lay it in the praetor's chair,

Where Brutus may but find it; and throw this

In at his window; set this up with wax

Upon old Brutus' statue: all this done,

Repair to Pompey's Porch, where you shall find us.

Is Decius Brutus and Trebonius there?

CINNA.

All but Metellus Cimber, and he's gone

To seek you at your house. Well, I will hie,

And so bestow these papers as you bade me.

CASSIUS.

That done, repair to Pompey's theatre.

[Exit Cinna.]

Come, Casca, you and I will yet, ere day,

See Brutus at his house: three parts of him

Is ours already, and the man entire

Upon the next encounter, yields him ours.

CASCA.

O, he sits high in all the people's hearts!

And that which would appear offence in us,

His countenance, like richest alchemy,

Will change to virtue and to worthiness.

CASSIUS.

Him, and his worth, and our great need of him,

You have right well conceited. Let us go,

For it is after midnight; and ere day,

We will awake him, and be sure of him.

[Exeunt.]

ACT II

SCENE I. Rome. Brutus' orchard.

Enter Brutus.

BRUTUS.

What, Lucius, ho!

I cannot, by the progress of the stars,

Give guess how near to day.—Lucius, I say!

I would it were my fault to sleep so soundly.

When, Lucius, when? Awake, I say! What, Lucius!

Enter Lucius.

LUCIUS.

Call'd you, my lord?

BRUTUS.

Get me a taper in my study, Lucius:

When it is lighted, come and call me here.

LUCIUS.

I will, my lord.

[Exit.]

BRUTUS.

It must be by his death: and for my part,

I know no personal cause to spurn at him,

But for the general. He would be crown'd:

How that might change his nature, there's the question.

It is the bright day that brings forth the adder,

And that craves wary walking. Crown him?—that;

And then, I grant, we put a sting in him,

That at his will he may do danger with.

Th' abuse of greatness is, when it disjoins

Remorse from power; and, to speak truth of Caesar,

I have not known when his affections sway'd

More than his reason. But 'tis a common proof,

That lowliness is young ambition's ladder,

Whereto the climber-upward turns his face;

But when he once attains the upmost round,

He then unto the ladder turns his back,

Looks in the clouds, scorning the base degrees

By which he did ascend. So Caesar may;

Then lest he may, prevent. And since the quarrel

Will bear no colour for the thing he is,

Fashion it thus: that what he is, augmented,

Would run to these and these extremities:

And therefore think him as a serpent's egg

Which hatch'd, would, as his kind grow mischievous;

And kill him in the shell.

Enter Lucius.

LUCIUS.

The taper burneth in your closet, sir.

Searching the window for a flint, I found

This paper, thus seal'd up, and I am sure

It did not lie there when I went to bed.

[Gives him the letter.]

BRUTUS.

Get you to bed again; it is not day.

Is not tomorrow, boy, the Ides of March?

LUCIUS.

I know not, sir.

BRUTUS.

Look in the calendar, and bring me word.

LUCIUS.

I will, sir.

[Exit.]

BRUTUS.

The exhalations, whizzing in the air

Give so much light that I may read by them.

[Opens the letter and reads.]

Brutus, thou sleep'st: awake and see thyself.

Shall Rome, &c. Speak, strike, redress!

"Brutus, thou sleep'st: awake!"

45

Such instigations have been often dropp'd

Where I have took them up.

"Shall Rome, &c." Thus must I piece it out:

Shall Rome stand under one man's awe? What, Rome?

My ancestors did from the streets of Rome

The Tarquin drive, when he was call'd a king.

"Speak, strike, redress!" Am I entreated

To speak and strike? O Rome, I make thee promise,

If the redress will follow, thou receivest

Thy full petition at the hand of Brutus.

Enter Lucius.

LUCIUS.

Sir, March is wasted fifteen days.

[Knock within.]

BRUTUS.

'Tis good. Go to the gate, somebody knocks.

[Exit Lucius.]

Since Cassius first did whet me against Caesar,

I have not slept.

Between the acting of a dreadful thing

And the first motion, all the interim is

Like a phantasma, or a hideous dream:

The genius and the mortal instruments

Are then in council; and the state of man,

Like to a little kingdom, suffers then

The nature of an insurrection.

Enter Lucius.

LUCIUS.

Sir, 'tis your brother Cassius at the door,

Who doth desire to see you.

BRUTUS.

Is he alone?

LUCIUS.

No, sir, there are moe with him.

BRUTUS.

Do you know them?

LUCIUS.

No, sir, their hats are pluck'd about their ears,

And half their faces buried in their cloaks,

That by no means I may discover them

By any mark of favour.

BRUTUS.

Let 'em enter.

[Exit Lucius.]

They are the faction. O conspiracy,

Sham'st thou to show thy dangerous brow by night,

When evils are most free? O, then, by day

Where wilt thou find a cavern dark enough

To mask thy monstrous visage? Seek none, conspiracy;

Hide it in smiles and affability:

For if thou path, thy native semblance on,

Not Erebus itself were dim enough

To hide thee from prevention.

Enter Cassius, Casca, Decius, Cinna, Metellus Cimber and Trebonius.

CASSIUS.

I think we are too bold upon your rest:

Good morrow, Brutus; do we trouble you?

BRUTUS.

I have been up this hour, awake all night.

Know I these men that come along with you?

CASSIUS.

Yes, every man of them; and no man here

But honours you; and everyone doth wish

You had but that opinion of yourself

Which every noble Roman bears of you.

This is Trebonius.

BRUTUS.

He is welcome hither.

CASSIUS.

This Decius Brutus.

BRUTUS.

He is welcome too.

CASSIUS.

This, Casca; this, Cinna; and this, Metellus Cimber.

BRUTUS.

They are all welcome.

What watchful cares do interpose themselves

Betwixt your eyes and night?

CASSIUS.

Shall I entreat a word?

[They whisper.]

DECIUS.

Here lies the east: doth not the day break here?

CASCA.

No.

CINNA.

O, pardon, sir, it doth; and yon grey lines

That fret the clouds are messengers of day.

CASCA.

You shall confess that you are both deceiv'd.

Here, as I point my sword, the Sun arises;

Which is a great way growing on the South,

Weighing the youthful season of the year.

Some two months hence, up higher toward the North

He first presents his fire; and the high East

Stands, as the Capitol, directly here.

BRUTUS.

Give me your hands all over, one by one.

CASSIUS.

And let us swear our resolution.

BRUTUS.

No, not an oath. If not the face of men,

The sufferance of our souls, the time's abuse—

If these be motives weak, break off betimes,

And every man hence to his idle bed.

So let high-sighted tyranny range on,

Till each man drop by lottery. But if these,

As I am sure they do, bear fire enough

To kindle cowards, and to steel with valour

The melting spirits of women; then, countrymen,

What need we any spur but our own cause

To prick us to redress? what other bond

Than secret Romans, that have spoke the word,

And will not palter? and what other oath

Than honesty to honesty engag'd,

That this shall be, or we will fall for it?

Swear priests and cowards, and men cautelous,

Old feeble carrions, and such suffering souls

That welcome wrongs; unto bad causes swear

Such creatures as men doubt; but do not stain

The even virtue of our enterprise,

Nor th' insuppressive mettle of our spirits,

To think that or our cause or our performance

Did need an oath; when every drop of blood

That every Roman bears, and nobly bears,

Is guilty of a several bastardy,

If he do break the smallest particle

Of any promise that hath pass'd from him.

CASSIUS.

But what of Cicero? Shall we sound him?

I think he will stand very strong with us.

CASCA.

Let us not leave him out.

CINNA.

No, by no means.

METELLUS.

O, let us have him, for his silver hairs

Will purchase us a good opinion,

And buy men's voices to commend our deeds.

It shall be said, his judgment rul'd our hands;

Our youths and wildness shall no whit appear,

But all be buried in his gravity.

BRUTUS.

O, name him not; let us not break with him;

For he will never follow anything

That other men begin.

CASSIUS.

Then leave him out.

CASCA.

Indeed, he is not fit.

DECIUS.

Shall no man else be touch'd but only Caesar?

CASSIUS.

Decius, well urg'd. I think it is not meet,

Mark Antony, so well belov'd of Caesar,

Should outlive Caesar: we shall find of him

A shrewd contriver; and you know, his means,

If he improve them, may well stretch so far

As to annoy us all; which to prevent,

Let Antony and Caesar fall together.

BRUTUS.

Our course will seem too bloody, Caius Cassius,

To cut the head off, and then hack the limbs,

Like wrath in death, and envy afterwards;

For Antony is but a limb of Caesar.

Let us be sacrificers, but not butchers, Caius.

We all stand up against the spirit of Caesar,

And in the spirit of men there is no blood.

O, that we then could come by Caesar's spirit,

And not dismember Caesar! But, alas,

Caesar must bleed for it! And, gentle friends,

Let's kill him boldly, but not wrathfully;

Let's carve him as a dish fit for the gods,

Not hew him as a carcass fit for hounds.

And let our hearts, as subtle masters do,

Stir up their servants to an act of rage,

And after seem to chide 'em. This shall mark

Our purpose necessary, and not envious;

Which so appearing to the common eyes,

We shall be call'd purgers, not murderers.

And for Mark Antony, think not of him;

For he can do no more than Caesar's arm

When Caesar's head is off.

CASSIUS.

Yet I fear him;

For in the ingrafted love he bears to Caesar—

BRUTUS.

Alas, good Cassius, do not think of him:

If he love Caesar, all that he can do

Is to himself; take thought and die for Caesar.

And that were much he should; for he is given

To sports, to wildness, and much company.

TREBONIUS.

There is no fear in him; let him not die;

For he will live, and laugh at this hereafter.

[Clock strikes.]

BRUTUS.

Peace! count the clock.

CASSIUS.

The clock hath stricken three.

TREBONIUS.

'Tis time to part.

CASSIUS.

But it is doubtful yet

Whether Caesar will come forth today or no;

For he is superstitious grown of late,

Quite from the main opinion he held once

Of fantasy, of dreams, and ceremonies.

It may be these apparent prodigies,

The unaccustom'd terror of this night,

And the persuasion of his augurers,

May hold him from the Capitol today.

DECIUS.

Never fear that: if he be so resolved,

I can o'ersway him, for he loves to hear

That unicorns may be betray'd with trees,

And bears with glasses, elephants with holes,

Lions with toils, and men with flatterers.

But when I tell him he hates flatterers,

He says he does, being then most flattered.

Let me work;

For I can give his humour the true bent,

And I will bring him to the Capitol.

CASSIUS.

Nay, we will all of us be there to fetch him.

BRUTUS.

By the eighth hour: is that the uttermost?

CINNA.

Be that the uttermost; and fail not then.

METELLUS.

Caius Ligarius doth bear Caesar hard,

Who rated him for speaking well of Pompey;

I wonder none of you have thought of him.

BRUTUS.

Now, good Metellus, go along by him:

He loves me well, and I have given him reason;

Send him but hither, and I'll fashion him.

CASSIUS.

The morning comes upon's. We'll leave you, Brutus.

And, friends, disperse yourselves; but all remember

What you have said, and show yourselves true Romans.

BRUTUS.

Good gentlemen, look fresh and merrily;

Let not our looks put on our purposes,

But bear it as our Roman actors do,

With untired spirits and formal constancy.

And so, good morrow to you everyone.

[Exeunt all but Brutus.]

Boy! Lucius! Fast asleep? It is no matter;

Enjoy the honey-heavy dew of slumber:

Thou hast no figures nor no fantasies,

Which busy care draws in the brains of men;

Therefore thou sleep'st so sound.

Enter Portia.

PORTIA.

Brutus, my lord.

BRUTUS.

Portia, what mean you? Wherefore rise you now?

It is not for your health thus to commit

Your weak condition to the raw cold morning.

PORTIA.

Nor for yours neither. Y' have ungently, Brutus,

Stole from my bed; and yesternight at supper,

You suddenly arose, and walk'd about,

Musing and sighing, with your arms across;

And when I ask'd you what the matter was,

You star'd upon me with ungentle looks.

I urg'd you further; then you scratch'd your head,

And too impatiently stamp'd with your foot;

Yet I insisted, yet you answer'd not,

But with an angry wafture of your hand

Gave sign for me to leave you. So I did,

Fearing to strengthen that impatience

Which seem'd too much enkindled; and withal

Hoping it was but an effect of humour,

Which sometime hath his hour with every man.

It will not let you eat, nor talk, nor sleep;

And could it work so much upon your shape

As it hath much prevail'd on your condition,

I should not know you, Brutus. Dear my lord,

Make me acquainted with your cause of grief.

BRUTUS.

I am not well in health, and that is all.

PORTIA.

Brutus is wise, and, were he not in health,

He would embrace the means to come by it.

BRUTUS.

Why, so I do. Good Portia, go to bed.

PORTIA.

Is Brutus sick, and is it physical

To walk unbraced and suck up the humours

Of the dank morning? What, is Brutus sick,

And will he steal out of his wholesome bed

To dare the vile contagion of the night,

And tempt the rheumy and unpurged air

To add unto his sickness? No, my Brutus;

You have some sick offence within your mind,

Which, by the right and virtue of my place,

I ought to know of: and, upon my knees,

I charm you, by my once commended beauty,

By all your vows of love, and that great vow

Which did incorporate and make us one,

That you unfold to me, your self, your half,

Why you are heavy, and what men tonight

Have had resort to you; for here have been

Some six or seven, who did hide their faces

Even from darkness.

BRUTUS.

Kneel not, gentle Portia.

PORTIA.

I should not need, if you were gentle Brutus.

Within the bond of marriage, tell me, Brutus,

Is it excepted I should know no secrets

That appertain to you? Am I your self

But, as it were, in sort or limitation,

To keep with you at meals, comfort your bed,

And talk to you sometimes? Dwell I but in the suburbs

Of your good pleasure? If it be no more,

Portia is Brutus' harlot, not his wife.

BRUTUS.

You are my true and honourable wife,

As dear to me as are the ruddy drops

That visit my sad heart.

PORTIA.

If this were true, then should I know this secret.

I grant I am a woman; but withal

A woman that Lord Brutus took to wife;

I grant I am a woman; but withal

A woman well reputed, Cato's daughter.

Think you I am no stronger than my sex,

Being so father'd and so husbanded?

Tell me your counsels, I will not disclose 'em.

I have made strong proof of my constancy,

Giving myself a voluntary wound

Here, in the thigh: can I bear that with patience

And not my husband's secrets?

BRUTUS.

O ye gods,

Render me worthy of this noble wife!

[Knock.]

Hark, hark, one knocks. Portia, go in awhile;

And by and by thy bosom shall partake

The secrets of my heart.

All my engagements I will construe to thee,

All the charactery of my sad brows.

Leave me with haste.

[Exit Portia.]

Enter Lucius with Ligarius.

Lucius, who's that knocks?

LUCIUS.

Here is a sick man that would speak with you.

BRUTUS.

Caius Ligarius, that Metellus spake of.

Boy, stand aside. Caius Ligarius, how?

LIGARIUS.

Vouchsafe good-morrow from a feeble tongue.

BRUTUS.

O, what a time have you chose out, brave Caius,

To wear a kerchief! Would you were not sick!

LIGARIUS.

I am not sick, if Brutus have in hand

Any exploit worthy the name of honour.

BRUTUS.

Such an exploit have I in hand, Ligarius,

Had you a healthful ear to hear of it.

LIGARIUS.

By all the gods that Romans bow before,

I here discard my sickness. Soul of Rome!

Brave son, derived from honourable loins!

Thou, like an exorcist, hast conjur'd up

My mortified spirit. Now bid me run,

And I will strive with things impossible,

Yea, get the better of them. What's to do?

BRUTUS.

A piece of work that will make sick men whole.

LIGARIUS.

But are not some whole that we must make sick?

BRUTUS.

That must we also. What it is, my Caius,

I shall unfold to thee, as we are going,

To whom it must be done.

LIGARIUS.

Set on your foot,

And with a heart new-fir'd I follow you,

To do I know not what; but it sufficeth

That Brutus leads me on.

[Thunder.]

BRUTUS.

Follow me then.

[Exeunt.]

SCENE II. A room in Caesar's palace.

Thunder and lightning. Enter Caesar, in his nightgown.

CAESAR.

Nor heaven nor earth have been at peace tonight:

Thrice hath Calphurnia in her sleep cried out,

"Help, ho! They murder Caesar!" Who's within?

Enter a Servant.

SERVANT.

My lord?

CAESAR.

Go bid the priests do present sacrifice,

And bring me their opinions of success.

SERVANT.

I will, my lord.

[Exit.]

Enter Calphurnia.

CALPHURNIA.

What mean you, Caesar? Think you to walk forth?

You shall not stir out of your house today.

CAESAR.

Caesar shall forth. The things that threaten'd me

Ne'er look'd but on my back; when they shall see

The face of Caesar, they are vanished.

CALPHURNIA.

Caesar, I never stood on ceremonies,

Yet now they fright me. There is one within,

Besides the things that we have heard and seen,

Recounts most horrid sights seen by the watch.

A lioness hath whelped in the streets,

And graves have yawn'd, and yielded up their dead;

Fierce fiery warriors fight upon the clouds

In ranks and squadrons and right form of war,

Which drizzled blood upon the Capitol;

The noise of battle hurtled in the air,

Horses did neigh, and dying men did groan,

And ghosts did shriek and squeal about the streets.

O Caesar, these things are beyond all use,

And I do fear them!

CAESAR.

What can be avoided

Whose end is purpos'd by the mighty gods?

Yet Caesar shall go forth; for these predictions

Are to the world in general as to Caesar.

CALPHURNIA.

When beggars die, there are no comets seen;

The heavens themselves blaze forth the death of princes.

CAESAR.

Cowards die many times before their deaths;

The valiant never taste of death but once.

Of all the wonders that I yet have heard,

It seems to me most strange that men should fear,

Seeing that death, a necessary end,

Will come when it will come.

Enter Servant.

What say the augurers?

SERVANT.

They would not have you to stir forth today.

Plucking the entrails of an offering forth,

They could not find a heart within the beast.

CAESAR.

The gods do this in shame of cowardice:

Caesar should be a beast without a heart

If he should stay at home today for fear.

No, Caesar shall not. Danger knows full well

That Caesar is more dangerous than he.

We are two lions litter'd in one day,

And I the elder and more terrible,

And Caesar shall go forth.

CALPHURNIA.

Alas, my lord,

Your wisdom is consum'd in confidence.

Do not go forth today: call it my fear

That keeps you in the house, and not your own.

We'll send Mark Antony to the Senate-house,

And he shall say you are not well today.

Let me upon my knee prevail in this.

CAESAR.

Mark Antony shall say I am not well,

And for thy humour, I will stay at home.

Enter Decius.

Here's Decius Brutus, he shall tell them so.

DECIUS.

Caesar, all hail! Good morrow, worthy Caesar.

I come to fetch you to the Senate-house.

CAESAR.

And you are come in very happy time

To bear my greeting to the Senators,

And tell them that I will not come today.

Cannot, is false; and that I dare not, falser:

I will not come today. Tell them so, Decius.

CALPHURNIA.

Say he is sick.

CAESAR.

Shall Caesar send a lie?

Have I in conquest stretch'd mine arm so far,

To be afeard to tell grey-beards the truth?

Decius, go tell them Caesar will not come.

DECIUS.

Most mighty Caesar, let me know some cause,

Lest I be laugh'd at when I tell them so.

CAESAR.

The cause is in my will; I will not come.

That is enough to satisfy the Senate.

But for your private satisfaction,

Because I love you, I will let you know:

Calphurnia here, my wife, stays me at home.

She dreamt tonight she saw my statue,

Which like a fountain with an hundred spouts

Did run pure blood; and many lusty Romans

Came smiling, and did bathe their hands in it.

And these does she apply for warnings and portents

And evils imminent; and on her knee

Hath begg'd that I will stay at home today.

DECIUS.

This dream is all amiss interpreted:

It was a vision fair and fortunate.

Your statue spouting blood in many pipes,

In which so many smiling Romans bath'd,

Signifies that from you great Rome shall suck

Reviving blood, and that great men shall press

For tinctures, stains, relics, and cognizance.

This by Calphurnia's dream is signified.

CAESAR.

And this way have you well expounded it.

DECIUS.

I have, when you have heard what I can say;

And know it now. The Senate have concluded

To give this day a crown to mighty Caesar.

If you shall send them word you will not come,

Their minds may change. Besides, it were a mock

Apt to be render'd, for someone to say,

"Break up the Senate till another time,

When Caesar's wife shall meet with better dreams."

If Caesar hide himself, shall they not whisper

"Lo, Caesar is afraid"?

Pardon me, Caesar; for my dear dear love

To your proceeding bids me tell you this,

And reason to my love is liable.

CAESAR.

How foolish do your fears seem now, Calphurnia!

I am ashamed I did yield to them.

Give me my robe, for I will go.

Enter Brutus, Ligarius, Metellus, Casca, Trebonius, Cinna and Publius.

And look where Publius is come to fetch me.

PUBLIUS.

Good morrow, Caesar.

CAESAR.

Welcome, Publius.

What, Brutus, are you stirr'd so early too?

Good morrow, Casca. Caius Ligarius,

Caesar was ne'er so much your enemy

As that same ague which hath made you lean.

What is't o'clock?

BRUTUS.

Caesar, 'tis strucken eight.

CAESAR.

I thank you for your pains and courtesy.

Enter Antony.

See! Antony, that revels long a-nights,

Is notwithstanding up. Good morrow, Antony.

ANTONY.

So to most noble Caesar.

CAESAR.

Bid them prepare within.

I am to blame to be thus waited for.

Now, Cinna; now, Metellus; what, Trebonius!

I have an hour's talk in store for you:

Remember that you call on me today;

Be near me, that I may remember you.

TREBONIUS.

Caesar, I will. [Aside.] and so near will I be,

That your best friends shall wish I had been further.

CAESAR.

Good friends, go in, and taste some wine with me;

And we, like friends, will straightway go together.

BRUTUS.

[Aside.] That every like is not the same, O Caesar,

The heart of Brutus yearns to think upon.

[Exeunt.]

SCENE III. A street near the Capitol.

Enter Artemidorus, reading a paper.

ARTEMIDORUS.

"Caesar, beware of Brutus; take heed of Cassius; come not near Casca; have an eye to Cinna; trust not Trebonius; mark well Metellus Cimber; Decius Brutus loves thee not; thou hast wrong'd Caius Ligarius. There is but one mind in all these men, and it is bent against Caesar. If thou be'st not immortal, look about you: security gives way to conspiracy. The mighty gods defend thee!

Thy lover, Artemidorus."

Here will I stand till Caesar pass along,

And as a suitor will I give him this.

My heart laments that virtue cannot live

Out of the teeth of emulation.

If thou read this, O Caesar, thou mayest live;

If not, the Fates with traitors do contrive.

[Exit.]

SCENE IV. Another part of the same street, before the house of Brutus.

Enter Portia and Lucius.

PORTIA.

I pr'ythee, boy, run to the Senate-house;

Stay not to answer me, but get thee gone.

Why dost thou stay?

LUCIUS.

To know my errand, madam.

PORTIA.

I would have had thee there and here again,

Ere I can tell thee what thou shouldst do there.

[Aside.] O constancy, be strong upon my side,

Set a huge mountain 'tween my heart and tongue!

I have a man's mind, but a woman's might.

How hard it is for women to keep counsel!

Art thou here yet?

LUCIUS.

Madam, what should I do?

Run to the Capitol, and nothing else?

And so return to you, and nothing else?

PORTIA.

Yes, bring me word, boy, if thy lord look well,

For he went sickly forth: and take good note

What Caesar doth, what suitors press to him.

Hark, boy, what noise is that?

LUCIUS.

I hear none, madam.

PORTIA.

Pr'ythee, listen well.

I heard a bustling rumour, like a fray,

And the wind brings it from the Capitol.

LUCIUS.

Sooth, madam, I hear nothing.

Enter the Soothsayer.

PORTIA.

Come hither, fellow:

Which way hast thou been?

SOOTHSAYER.

At mine own house, good lady.

PORTIA.

What is't o'clock?

SOOTHSAYER.

About the ninth hour, lady.

PORTIA.

Is Caesar yet gone to the Capitol?

SOOTHSAYER.

Madam, not yet. I go to take my stand,

To see him pass on to the Capitol.

PORTIA.

Thou hast some suit to Caesar, hast thou not?

SOOTHSAYER.

That I have, lady, if it will please Caesar

To be so good to Caesar as to hear me,

I shall beseech him to befriend himself.

PORTIA.

Why, know'st thou any harm's intended towards him?

SOOTHSAYER.

None that I know will be, much that I fear may chance.

Good morrow to you. Here the street is narrow.

The throng that follows Caesar at the heels,

Of Senators, of Praetors, common suitors,

Will crowd a feeble man almost to death:

I'll get me to a place more void, and there

Speak to great Caesar as he comes along.

[Exit.]

PORTIA.

I must go in.

[Aside.] Ay me, how weak a thing

The heart of woman is! O Brutus,

The heavens speed thee in thine enterprise!

Sure, the boy heard me. Brutus hath a suit

That Caesar will not grant. O, I grow faint.

Run, Lucius, and commend me to my lord;

Say I am merry; come to me again,

And bring me word what he doth say to thee.

[Exeunt.]

ACT III

SCENE I. Rome. Before the Capitol; the Senate sitting.

A crowd of people in the street leading to the Capitol. Flourish. Enter Caesar, Brutus, Cassius, Casca, Decius, Metellus, Trebonius, Cinna, Antony, Lepidus, Artemidorus, Publius, Popilius and the Soothsayer.

CAESAR.

The Ides of March are come.

SOOTHSAYER.

Ay, Caesar; but not gone.

ARTEMIDORUS.

Hail, Caesar! Read this schedule.

DECIUS.

Trebonius doth desire you to o'er-read,

At your best leisure, this his humble suit.

ARTEMIDORUS.

O Caesar, read mine first; for mine's a suit

That touches Caesar nearer. Read it, great Caesar.

CAESAR.

What touches us ourself shall be last serv'd.

ARTEMIDORUS.

Delay not, Caesar. Read it instantly.

CAESAR.

What, is the fellow mad?

PUBLIUS.

Sirrah, give place.

CASSIUS.

What, urge you your petitions in the street?

Come to the Capitol.

Caesar enters the Capitol, the rest following. All the Senators rise.

POPILIUS.

I wish your enterprise today may thrive.

CASSIUS.

What enterprise, Popilius?

POPILIUS.

Fare you well.

[Advances to Caesar.]

BRUTUS.

What said Popilius Lena?

CASSIUS.

He wish'd today our enterprise might thrive.

I fear our purpose is discovered.

BRUTUS.

Look how he makes to Caesar: mark him.

CASSIUS.

Casca, be sudden, for we fear prevention.

Brutus, what shall be done? If this be known,

Cassius or Caesar never shall turn back,

For I will slay myself.

BRUTUS.

Cassius, be constant:

Popilius Lena speaks not of our purposes;

For look, he smiles, and Caesar doth not change.

CASSIUS.

Trebonius knows his time, for look you, Brutus,

He draws Mark Antony out of the way.

     [Exeunt Antony and Trebonius. Caesar and the Senators take their
                      seats.]

DECIUS.

Where is Metellus Cimber? Let him go,

And presently prefer his suit to Caesar.

BRUTUS.

He is address'd; press near and second him.

CINNA.

Casca, you are the first that rears your hand.

CAESAR.

Are we all ready? What is now amiss

That Caesar and his Senate must redress?

METELLUS.

Most high, most mighty, and most puissant Caesar,

Metellus Cimber throws before thy seat

An humble heart.

[Kneeling.]

CAESAR.

I must prevent thee, Cimber.

These couchings and these lowly courtesies

Might fire the blood of ordinary men,

And turn pre-ordinance and first decree

Into the law of children. Be not fond,

To think that Caesar bears such rebel blood

That will be thaw'd from the true quality

With that which melteth fools; I mean sweet words,

Low-crooked curtsies, and base spaniel fawning.

Thy brother by decree is banished:

If thou dost bend, and pray, and fawn for him,

I spurn thee like a cur out of my way.

Know, Caesar dost not wrong, nor without cause

Will he be satisfied.

METELLUS.

Is there no voice more worthy than my own,

To sound more sweetly in great Caesar's ear

For the repealing of my banish'd brother?

BRUTUS.

I kiss thy hand, but not in flattery, Caesar;

Desiring thee that Publius Cimber may

Have an immediate freedom of repeal.

CAESAR.

What, Brutus?

CASSIUS.

Pardon, Caesar; Caesar, pardon:

As low as to thy foot doth Cassius fall,

To beg enfranchisement for Publius Cimber.

CAESAR.

I could be well mov'd, if I were as you;

If I could pray to move, prayers would move me:

But I am constant as the northern star,

Of whose true-fix'd and resting quality

There is no fellow in the firmament.

The skies are painted with unnumber'd sparks,

They are all fire, and every one doth shine;

But there's but one in all doth hold his place.

So in the world; 'tis furnish'd well with men,

And men are flesh and blood, and apprehensive;

Yet in the number I do know but one

That unassailable holds on his rank,

Unshak'd of motion: and that I am he,

Let me a little show it, even in this,

That I was constant Cimber should be banish'd,

And constant do remain to keep him so.

CINNA.

O Caesar,—

CAESAR.

Hence! wilt thou lift up Olympus?

DECIUS.

Great Caesar,—

CAESAR.

Doth not Brutus bootless kneel?

CASCA.

Speak, hands, for me!

[Casca stabs Caesar in the neck. Caesar catches hold of his arm. He is then stabbed by several other Conspirators, and at last by Marcus Brutus.]

CAESAR.

Et tu, Brute?—Then fall, Caesar!

[Dies. The Senators and People retire in confusion.]

CINNA.

Liberty! Freedom! Tyranny is dead!

Run hence, proclaim, cry it about the streets.

CASSIUS.

Some to the common pulpits and cry out,

"Liberty, freedom, and enfranchisement!"

BRUTUS.

People and Senators, be not affrighted.

Fly not; stand still; ambition's debt is paid.

CASCA.

Go to the pulpit, Brutus.

DECIUS.

And Cassius too.

BRUTUS.

Where's Publius?

CINNA.

Here, quite confounded with this mutiny.

METELLUS.

Stand fast together, lest some friend of Caesar's

Should chance—

BRUTUS.

Talk not of standing. Publius, good cheer!

There is no harm intended to your person,

Nor to no Roman else. So tell them, Publius.

CASSIUS.

And leave us, Publius; lest that the people

Rushing on us, should do your age some mischief.

BRUTUS.

Do so; and let no man abide this deed

But we the doers.

Enter Trebonius.

CASSIUS.

Where's Antony?

TREBONIUS.

Fled to his house amaz'd.

Men, wives, and children stare, cry out, and run,

As it were doomsday.

BRUTUS.

Fates, we will know your pleasures.

That we shall die, we know; 'tis but the time

And drawing days out, that men stand upon.

CASCA.

Why, he that cuts off twenty years of life

Cuts off so many years of fearing death.

BRUTUS.

Grant that, and then is death a benefit:

So are we Caesar's friends, that have abridg'd

His time of fearing death. Stoop, Romans, stoop,

And let us bathe our hands in Caesar's blood

Up to the elbows, and besmear our swords:

Then walk we forth, even to the market-place,

And waving our red weapons o'er our heads,

Let's all cry, "Peace, freedom, and liberty!"

CASSIUS.

Stoop then, and wash. How many ages hence

Shall this our lofty scene be acted over

In States unborn, and accents yet unknown!

BRUTUS.

How many times shall Caesar bleed in sport,

That now on Pompey's basis lies along,

No worthier than the dust!

CASSIUS.

So oft as that shall be,

So often shall the knot of us be call'd

The men that gave their country liberty.

DECIUS.

What, shall we forth?

CASSIUS.

Ay, every man away.

Brutus shall lead; and we will grace his heels

With the most boldest and best hearts of Rome.

Enter a Servant.

BRUTUS.

Soft, who comes here? A friend of Antony's.

SERVANT.

Thus, Brutus, did my master bid me kneel;

Thus did Mark Antony bid me fall down;

And, being prostrate, thus he bade me say:

Brutus is noble, wise, valiant, and honest;

Caesar was mighty, bold, royal, and loving;

Say I love Brutus and I honour him;

Say I fear'd Caesar, honour'd him, and lov'd him.

If Brutus will vouchsafe that Antony

May safely come to him, and be resolv'd

How Caesar hath deserv'd to lie in death,

Mark Antony shall not love Caesar dead

So well as Brutus living; but will follow

The fortunes and affairs of noble Brutus

Thorough the hazards of this untrod state,

With all true faith. So says my master Antony.

BRUTUS.

Thy master is a wise and valiant Roman;

I never thought him worse.

Tell him, so please him come unto this place,

He shall be satisfied and, by my honour,

Depart untouch'd.

SERVANT.

I'll fetch him presently.

[Exit.]

BRUTUS.

I know that we shall have him well to friend.

85

CASSIUS.

I wish we may: but yet have I a mind

That fears him much; and my misgiving still

Falls shrewdly to the purpose.

Enter Antony.

BRUTUS.

But here comes Antony. Welcome, Mark Antony.

ANTONY.

O mighty Caesar! Dost thou lie so low?

Are all thy conquests, glories, triumphs, spoils,

Shrunk to this little measure? Fare thee well.

I know not, gentlemen, what you intend,

Who else must be let blood, who else is rank:

If I myself, there is no hour so fit

As Caesar's death's hour; nor no instrument

Of half that worth as those your swords, made rich

With the most noble blood of all this world.

I do beseech ye, if you bear me hard,

Now, whilst your purpled hands do reek and smoke,

Fulfill your pleasure. Live a thousand years,

I shall not find myself so apt to die.

No place will please me so, no means of death,

As here by Caesar, and by you cut off,

The choice and master spirits of this age.

BRUTUS.

O Antony, beg not your death of us.

Though now we must appear bloody and cruel,

As by our hands and this our present act

You see we do; yet see you but our hands

And this the bleeding business they have done.

Our hearts you see not; they are pitiful;

And pity to the general wrong of Rome—

As fire drives out fire, so pity pity—

Hath done this deed on Caesar. For your part,

To you our swords have leaden points, Mark Antony;

Our arms in strength of malice, and our hearts

Of brothers' temper, do receive you in

With all kind love, good thoughts, and reverence.

CASSIUS.

Your voice shall be as strong as any man's

In the disposing of new dignities.

BRUTUS.

Only be patient till we have appeas'd

The multitude, beside themselves with fear,

And then we will deliver you the cause

Why I, that did love Caesar when I struck him,

Have thus proceeded.

ANTONY.

I doubt not of your wisdom.

Let each man render me his bloody hand.

First, Marcus Brutus, will I shake with you;

Next, Caius Cassius, do I take your hand.

Now, Decius Brutus, yours; now yours, Metellus;

Yours, Cinna; and, my valiant Casca, yours;

Though last, not least in love, yours, good Trebonius.

Gentlemen all—alas, what shall I say?

My credit now stands on such slippery ground,

That one of two bad ways you must conceit me,

Either a coward or a flatterer.

That I did love thee, Caesar, O, 'tis true:

If then thy spirit look upon us now,

Shall it not grieve thee dearer than thy death,

To see thy Antony making his peace,

Shaking the bloody fingers of thy foes,

Most noble, in the presence of thy corse?

Had I as many eyes as thou hast wounds,

Weeping as fast as they stream forth thy blood,

It would become me better than to close

In terms of friendship with thine enemies.

Pardon me, Julius! Here wast thou bay'd, brave hart;

Here didst thou fall; and here thy hunters stand,

Sign'd in thy spoil, and crimson'd in thy lethe.

O world, thou wast the forest to this hart;

And this indeed, O world, the heart of thee.

How like a deer strucken by many princes,

Dost thou here lie!

CASSIUS.

Mark Antony,—

ANTONY.

Pardon me, Caius Cassius:

The enemies of Caesar shall say this;

Then, in a friend, it is cold modesty.

CASSIUS.

I blame you not for praising Caesar so;

But what compact mean you to have with us?

Will you be prick'd in number of our friends,

Or shall we on, and not depend on you?

ANTONY.

Therefore I took your hands; but was indeed

Sway'd from the point, by looking down on Caesar.

Friends am I with you all, and love you all,

Upon this hope, that you shall give me reasons

Why, and wherein, Caesar was dangerous.

BRUTUS.

Or else were this a savage spectacle.

Our reasons are so full of good regard

That were you, Antony, the son of Caesar,

You should be satisfied.

ANTONY.

That's all I seek,

And am moreover suitor that I may

Produce his body to the market-place;

And in the pulpit, as becomes a friend,

Speak in the order of his funeral.

BRUTUS.

You shall, Mark Antony.

CASSIUS.

Brutus, a word with you.

[Aside to Brutus.] You know not what you do. Do not consent

That Antony speak in his funeral.

Know you how much the people may be mov'd

By that which he will utter?

BRUTUS.

[Aside to Cassius.] By your pardon:

I will myself into the pulpit first,

And show the reason of our Caesar's death.

What Antony shall speak, I will protest

He speaks by leave and by permission;

And that we are contented Caesar shall

Have all true rights and lawful ceremonies.

It shall advantage more than do us wrong.

CASSIUS.

[Aside to Brutus.] I know not what may fall; I like it not.

BRUTUS.

Mark Antony, here, take you Caesar's body.

You shall not in your funeral speech blame us,

But speak all good you can devise of Caesar,

And say you do't by our permission;

Else shall you not have any hand at all

About his funeral. And you shall speak

In the same pulpit whereto I am going,

After my speech is ended.

ANTONY.

Be it so;

I do desire no more.

BRUTUS.

Prepare the body, then, and follow us.

[Exeunt all but Antony.]

ANTONY.

O, pardon me, thou bleeding piece of earth,

That I am meek and gentle with these butchers.

Thou art the ruins of the noblest man

That ever lived in the tide of times.

Woe to the hand that shed this costly blood!

Over thy wounds now do I prophesy,

Which, like dumb mouths do ope their ruby lips

To beg the voice and utterance of my tongue,

A curse shall light upon the limbs of men;

Domestic fury and fierce civil strife

Shall cumber all the parts of Italy;

Blood and destruction shall be so in use,

And dreadful objects so familiar,

That mothers shall but smile when they behold

Their infants quartered with the hands of war;

All pity chok'd with custom of fell deeds:

And Caesar's spirit, ranging for revenge,

With Ate by his side come hot from Hell,

Shall in these confines with a monarch's voice

Cry havoc and let slip the dogs of war,

That this foul deed shall smell above the earth

With carrion men, groaning for burial.

Enter a Servant.

You serve Octavius Caesar, do you not?

SERVANT.

I do, Mark Antony.

ANTONY.

Caesar did write for him to come to Rome.

SERVANT.

He did receive his letters, and is coming,

And bid me say to you by word of mouth,—

[Seeing the body.] O Caesar!

ANTONY.

Thy heart is big, get thee apart and weep.

Passion, I see, is catching; for mine eyes,

Seeing those beads of sorrow stand in thine,

Began to water. Is thy master coming?

SERVANT.

He lies tonight within seven leagues of Rome.

ANTONY.

Post back with speed, and tell him what hath chanc'd.

Here is a mourning Rome, a dangerous Rome,

No Rome of safety for Octavius yet.

Hie hence, and tell him so. Yet stay awhile;

Thou shalt not back till I have borne this corse

Into the market-place: there shall I try,

In my oration, how the people take

The cruel issue of these bloody men;

According to the which thou shalt discourse

To young Octavius of the state of things.

Lend me your hand.

[Exeunt with Caesar's body.]

SCENE II. The same. The Forum.

Enter Brutus and goes into the pulpit, and Cassius, with a throng of Citizens.

CITIZENS.

We will be satisfied; let us be satisfied.

BRUTUS.

Then follow me, and give me audience, friends.

Cassius, go you into the other street

And part the numbers.

Those that will hear me speak, let 'em stay here;

Those that will follow Cassius, go with him;

And public reasons shall be rendered

Of Caesar's death.

FIRST CITIZEN.

I will hear Brutus speak.

SECOND CITIZEN.

I will hear Cassius; and compare their reasons,

When severally we hear them rendered.

[Exit Cassius, with some of the Citizens. Brutus goes into the rostrum.]

THIRD CITIZEN.

The noble Brutus is ascended: silence!

BRUTUS.

Be patient till the last.

Romans, countrymen, and lovers, hear me for my cause; and be silent, that you may hear. Believe me for mine honour, and have respect to mine honour, that you may believe. Censure me in your wisdom, and awake your senses, that you may the better judge. If there be any in this assembly, any dear friend of Caesar's, to him I say that Brutus' love to Caesar was no less than his. If then that friend demand why Brutus rose against Caesar, this is my answer: Not that I loved Caesar less, but that I loved Rome more. Had you rather Caesar were living, and die all slaves, than that Caesar were dead, to live all free men? As Caesar loved me, I weep for him; as he was fortunate, I rejoice at it; as he was valiant, I honour him; but, as he was ambitious, I slew him. There is tears, for his love; joy for his fortune; honour for his valour; and death, for his ambition. Who is here so base, that would be a bondman? If any, speak; for him have I offended. Who is here so rude, that would not be a Roman? If any, speak; for him have I offended. Who is here so vile, that will not love his country? If any, speak; for him have I offended. I pause for a reply.

CITIZENS.

None, Brutus, none.

BRUTUS.

Then none have I offended. I have done no more to Caesar than you shall do to Brutus. The question of his death is enroll'd in the Capitol, his glory not extenuated, wherein he was worthy; nor his offences enforc'd, for which he suffered death.

Enter Antony and others, with Caesar's body.

Here comes his body, mourned by Mark Antony, who, though he had no hand in his death, shall receive the benefit of his dying, a place in the commonwealth; as which of you shall not? With this I depart, that, as I slew my best lover for the good of Rome, I have the same dagger for myself, when it shall please my country to need my death.

CITIZENS.

Live, Brutus! live, live!

FIRST CITIZEN.

Bring him with triumph home unto his house.

SECOND CITIZEN.

Give him a statue with his ancestors.

THIRD CITIZEN.

Let him be Caesar.

FOURTH CITIZEN.

Caesar's better parts

Shall be crown'd in Brutus.

FIRST CITIZEN.

We'll bring him to his house with shouts and clamours.

BRUTUS.

My countrymen,—

SECOND CITIZEN.

Peace! Silence! Brutus speaks.

FIRST CITIZEN.

Peace, ho!

BRUTUS.

Good countrymen, let me depart alone,

And, for my sake, stay here with Antony.

Do grace to Caesar's corpse, and grace his speech

Tending to Caesar's glories, which Mark Antony,

By our permission, is allow'd to make.

I do entreat you, not a man depart,

Save I alone, till Antony have spoke.

[Exit.]

FIRST CITIZEN.

Stay, ho! and let us hear Mark Antony.

THIRD CITIZEN.

Let him go up into the public chair.

We'll hear him. Noble Antony, go up.

ANTONY.

For Brutus' sake, I am beholding to you.

[Goes up.]

FOURTH CITIZEN.

What does he say of Brutus?

THIRD CITIZEN.

He says, for Brutus' sake

He finds himself beholding to us all.

FOURTH CITIZEN.

'Twere best he speak no harm of Brutus here!

FIRST CITIZEN.

This Caesar was a tyrant.

THIRD CITIZEN.

Nay, that's certain.

We are blest that Rome is rid of him.

SECOND CITIZEN.

Peace! let us hear what Antony can say.

ANTONY.

You gentle Romans,—

CITIZENS.

Peace, ho! let us hear him.

ANTONY.

Friends, Romans, countrymen, lend me your ears;

I come to bury Caesar, not to praise him.

The evil that men do lives after them,

The good is oft interred with their bones;

So let it be with Caesar. The noble Brutus

Hath told you Caesar was ambitious.

If it were so, it was a grievous fault,

And grievously hath Caesar answer'd it.

Here, under leave of Brutus and the rest,

For Brutus is an honourable man,

So are they all, all honourable men,

Come I to speak in Caesar's funeral.

He was my friend, faithful and just to me;

But Brutus says he was ambitious,

And Brutus is an honourable man.

He hath brought many captives home to Rome,

Whose ransoms did the general coffers fill:

Did this in Caesar seem ambitious?

When that the poor have cried, Caesar hath wept;

Ambition should be made of sterner stuff:

Yet Brutus says he was ambitious;

And Brutus is an honourable man.

You all did see that on the Lupercal

I thrice presented him a kingly crown,

Which he did thrice refuse. Was this ambition?

Yet Brutus says he was ambitious;

And sure he is an honourable man.

I speak not to disprove what Brutus spoke,

But here I am to speak what I do know.

You all did love him once, not without cause;

What cause withholds you then to mourn for him?

O judgment, thou art fled to brutish beasts,

And men have lost their reason. Bear with me.

My heart is in the coffin there with Caesar,

And I must pause till it come back to me.

FIRST CITIZEN.

Methinks there is much reason in his sayings.

SECOND CITIZEN.

If thou consider rightly of the matter,

Caesar has had great wrong.

THIRD CITIZEN.

Has he, masters?

I fear there will a worse come in his place.

FOURTH CITIZEN.

Mark'd ye his words? He would not take the crown;

Therefore 'tis certain he was not ambitious.

FIRST CITIZEN.

If it be found so, some will dear abide it.

SECOND CITIZEN.

Poor soul, his eyes are red as fire with weeping.

THIRD CITIZEN.

There's not a nobler man in Rome than Antony.

FOURTH CITIZEN.

Now mark him; he begins again to speak.

ANTONY.

But yesterday the word of Caesar might

Have stood against the world; now lies he there,

And none so poor to do him reverence.

O masters! If I were dispos'd to stir

Your hearts and minds to mutiny and rage,

I should do Brutus wrong and Cassius wrong,

Who, you all know, are honourable men.

I will not do them wrong; I rather choose

To wrong the dead, to wrong myself and you,

Than I will wrong such honourable men.

But here's a parchment with the seal of Caesar,

I found it in his closet; 'tis his will:

Let but the commons hear this testament,

Which, pardon me, I do not mean to read,

And they would go and kiss dead Caesar's wounds,

And dip their napkins in his sacred blood;

Yea, beg a hair of him for memory,

And, dying, mention it within their wills,

Bequeathing it as a rich legacy

Unto their issue.

FOURTH CITIZEN.

We'll hear the will. Read it, Mark Antony.

CITIZENS.

The will, the will! We will hear Caesar's will.

ANTONY.

Have patience, gentle friends, I must not read it.

It is not meet you know how Caesar loved you.

You are not wood, you are not stones, but men;

And being men, hearing the will of Caesar,

It will inflame you, it will make you mad.

'Tis good you know not that you are his heirs;

For if you should, O, what would come of it?

FOURTH CITIZEN.

Read the will! We'll hear it, Antony;

You shall read us the will, Caesar's will!

ANTONY.

Will you be patient? Will you stay awhile?

I have o'ershot myself to tell you of it.

I fear I wrong the honourable men

Whose daggers have stabb'd Caesar; I do fear it.

FOURTH CITIZEN.

They were traitors. Honourable men!

CITIZENS.

The will! The testament!

SECOND CITIZEN.

They were villains, murderers. The will! Read the will!

ANTONY.

You will compel me then to read the will?

Then make a ring about the corpse of Caesar,

And let me show you him that made the will.

Shall I descend? and will you give me leave?

CITIZENS.

Come down.

SECOND CITIZEN.

Descend.

[He comes down.]

THIRD CITIZEN.

You shall have leave.

FOURTH CITIZEN.

A ring! Stand round.

FIRST CITIZEN.

Stand from the hearse, stand from the body.

SECOND CITIZEN.

Room for Antony, most noble Antony!

ANTONY.

Nay, press not so upon me; stand far off.

CITIZENS.

Stand back; room! bear back.

ANTONY.

If you have tears, prepare to shed them now.

You all do know this mantle. I remember

The first time ever Caesar put it on;

'Twas on a Summer's evening, in his tent,

That day he overcame the Nervii.

Look, in this place ran Cassius' dagger through:

See what a rent the envious Casca made:

Through this the well-beloved Brutus stabb'd;

And as he pluck'd his cursed steel away,

Mark how the blood of Caesar follow'd it,

As rushing out of doors, to be resolv'd

If Brutus so unkindly knock'd, or no;

For Brutus, as you know, was Caesar's angel.

Judge, O you gods, how dearly Caesar lov'd him.

This was the most unkindest cut of all;

For when the noble Caesar saw him stab,

Ingratitude, more strong than traitors' arms,

Quite vanquish'd him: then burst his mighty heart;

And in his mantle muffling up his face,

Even at the base of Pompey's statue

Which all the while ran blood, great Caesar fell.

O, what a fall was there, my countrymen!

Then I, and you, and all of us fell down,

Whilst bloody treason flourish'd over us.

O, now you weep; and I perceive you feel

The dint of pity. These are gracious drops.

Kind souls, what weep you when you but behold

Our Caesar's vesture wounded? Look you here,

Here is himself, marr'd, as you see, with traitors.

FIRST CITIZEN.

O piteous spectacle!

SECOND CITIZEN.

O noble Caesar!

THIRD CITIZEN.

O woeful day!

FOURTH CITIZEN.

O traitors, villains!

FIRST CITIZEN.

O most bloody sight!

SECOND CITIZEN.

We will be revenged.

CITIZENS.

Revenge,—about,—seek,—burn,—fire,—kill,—slay,—let not a traitor live!

ANTONY.

Stay, countrymen.

FIRST CITIZEN.

Peace there! Hear the noble Antony.

SECOND CITIZEN.

We'll hear him, we'll follow him, we'll die with him.

ANTONY.

Good friends, sweet friends, let me not stir you up

To such a sudden flood of mutiny.

They that have done this deed are honourable.

What private griefs they have, alas, I know not,

That made them do it. They're wise and honourable,

And will, no doubt, with reasons answer you.

I come not, friends, to steal away your hearts.

I am no orator, as Brutus is;

But, as you know me all, a plain blunt man,

That love my friend; and that they know full well

That gave me public leave to speak of him.

For I have neither wit, nor words, nor worth,

Action, nor utterance, nor the power of speech,

To stir men's blood. I only speak right on.

I tell you that which you yourselves do know,

Show you sweet Caesar's wounds, poor poor dumb mouths,

And bid them speak for me. But were I Brutus,

And Brutus Antony, there were an Antony

Would ruffle up your spirits, and put a tongue

In every wound of Caesar, that should move

The stones of Rome to rise and mutiny.

CITIZENS.

We'll mutiny.

FIRST CITIZEN.

We'll burn the house of Brutus.

THIRD CITIZEN.

Away, then! come, seek the conspirators.

ANTONY.

Yet hear me, countrymen; yet hear me speak.

CITIZENS.

Peace, ho! Hear Antony; most noble Antony.

ANTONY.

Why, friends, you go to do you know not what.

Wherein hath Caesar thus deserved your loves?

Alas, you know not; I must tell you then.

You have forgot the will I told you of.

CITIZENS.

Most true; the will!—let's stay, and hear the will.

ANTONY.

Here is the will, and under Caesar's seal.

To every Roman citizen he gives,

To every several man, seventy-five drachmas.

SECOND CITIZEN.

Most noble Caesar! We'll revenge his death.

THIRD CITIZEN.

O, royal Caesar!

ANTONY.

Hear me with patience.

CITIZENS.

Peace, ho!

ANTONY.

Moreover, he hath left you all his walks,

His private arbors, and new-planted orchards,

On this side Tiber; he hath left them you,

And to your heirs forever; common pleasures,

To walk abroad, and recreate yourselves.

Here was a Caesar! when comes such another?

FIRST CITIZEN.

Never, never. Come, away, away!

We'll burn his body in the holy place,

And with the brands fire the traitors' houses.

Take up the body.

SECOND CITIZEN.

Go, fetch fire.

THIRD CITIZEN.

Pluck down benches.

FOURTH CITIZEN.

Pluck down forms, windows, anything.

[Exeunt Citizens, with the body.]

ANTONY.

Now let it work. Mischief, thou art afoot,

Take thou what course thou wilt!

Enter a Servant.

How now, fellow?

SERVANT.

Sir, Octavius is already come to Rome.

ANTONY.

Where is he?

SERVANT.

He and Lepidus are at Caesar's house.

ANTONY.

And thither will I straight to visit him.

He comes upon a wish. Fortune is merry,

And in this mood will give us anything.

SERVANT.

I heard him say Brutus and Cassius

Are rid like madmen through the gates of Rome.

ANTONY.

Belike they had some notice of the people,

How I had moved them. Bring me to Octavius.

[Exeunt.]

SCENE III. The same. A street.

Enter Cinna, the poet, and after him the citizens.

CINNA.

I dreamt tonight that I did feast with Caesar,

And things unluckily charge my fantasy.

I have no will to wander forth of doors,

Yet something leads me forth.

FIRST CITIZEN.

What is your name?

SECOND CITIZEN.

Whither are you going?

THIRD CITIZEN.

Where do you dwell?

FOURTH CITIZEN.

Are you a married man or a bachelor?

SECOND CITIZEN.

Answer every man directly.

FIRST CITIZEN.

Ay, and briefly.

FOURTH CITIZEN.

Ay, and wisely.

THIRD CITIZEN.

Ay, and truly, you were best.

CINNA.

What is my name? Whither am I going? Where do I dwell? Am I a married man or a bachelor? Then, to answer every man directly and briefly, wisely and truly. Wisely I say I am a bachelor.

SECOND CITIZEN.

That's as much as to say they are fools that marry; you'll bear me a bang for that, I fear. Proceed, directly.

CINNA.

Directly, I am going to Caesar's funeral.

FIRST CITIZEN.

As a friend, or an enemy?

CINNA.

As a friend.

SECOND CITIZEN.

That matter is answered directly.

FOURTH CITIZEN.

For your dwelling, briefly.

CINNA.

Briefly, I dwell by the Capitol.

THIRD CITIZEN.

Your name, sir, truly.

CINNA.

Truly, my name is Cinna.

FIRST CITIZEN.

Tear him to pieces! He's a conspirator.

CINNA.

I am Cinna the poet, I am Cinna the poet.

FOURTH CITIZEN.

Tear him for his bad verses, tear him for his bad verses.

CINNA.

I am not Cinna the conspirator.

FOURTH CITIZEN.

It is no matter, his name's Cinna; pluck but his name out of his heart, and turn him going.

THIRD CITIZEN.

Tear him, tear him! Come; brands, ho! firebrands. To Brutus', to Cassius'; burn all. Some to Decius' house, and some to Casca's, some to Ligarius'. Away, go!

[Exeunt.]

ACT IV

SCENE I. Rome. A room in Antony's house.

Enter Antony, Octavius and Lepidus, seated at a table.

ANTONY.

These many then shall die; their names are prick'd.

OCTAVIUS.

Your brother too must die; consent you, Lepidus?

LEPIDUS.

I do consent,—

OCTAVIUS.

Prick him down, Antony.

LEPIDUS.

Upon condition Publius shall not live,

Who is your sister's son, Mark Antony.

ANTONY.

He shall not live; look, with a spot I damn him.

But, Lepidus, go you to Caesar's house;

Fetch the will hither, and we shall determine

How to cut off some charge in legacies.

LEPIDUS.

What, shall I find you here?

OCTAVIUS.

Or here, or at the Capitol.

[Exit Lepidus.]

ANTONY.

This is a slight unmeritable man,

Meet to be sent on errands. Is it fit,

The three-fold world divided, he should stand

One of the three to share it?

OCTAVIUS.

So you thought him,

And took his voice who should be prick'd to die

In our black sentence and proscription.

ANTONY.

Octavius, I have seen more days than you;

And though we lay these honours on this man,

To ease ourselves of divers sland'rous loads,

He shall but bear them as the ass bears gold,

To groan and sweat under the business,

Either led or driven, as we point the way;

And having brought our treasure where we will,

Then take we down his load, and turn him off,

Like to the empty ass, to shake his ears,

And graze in commons.

115

OCTAVIUS.

You may do your will;

But he's a tried and valiant soldier.

ANTONY.

So is my horse, Octavius; and for that

I do appoint him store of provender.

It is a creature that I teach to fight,

To wind, to stop, to run directly on,

His corporal motion govern'd by my spirit.

And, in some taste, is Lepidus but so:

He must be taught, and train'd, and bid go forth:

A barren-spirited fellow; one that feeds

On objects, arts, and imitations,

Which, out of use and stal'd by other men,

Begin his fashion. Do not talk of him

But as a property. And now, Octavius,

Listen great things. Brutus and Cassius

Are levying powers; we must straight make head.

Therefore let our alliance be combin'd,

Our best friends made, our means stretch'd;

And let us presently go sit in council,

How covert matters may be best disclos'd,

And open perils surest answered.

OCTAVIUS.

Let us do so: for we are at the stake,

And bay'd about with many enemies;

And some that smile have in their hearts, I fear,

Millions of mischiefs.

[Exeunt.]

SCENE II. Before Brutus' tent, in the camp near Sardis.

Drum. Enter Brutus, Lucilius, Titinius and Soldiers; Pindarus meeting them; Lucius at some distance.

BRUTUS.

Stand, ho!

LUCILIUS.

Give the word, ho! and stand.

BRUTUS.

What now, Lucilius! is Cassius near?

LUCILIUS.

He is at hand, and Pindarus is come

To do you salutation from his master.

[Pindarus gives a letter to Brutus.]

BRUTUS.

He greets me well. Your master, Pindarus,

In his own change, or by ill officers,

Hath given me some worthy cause to wish

Things done, undone: but, if he be at hand,

I shall be satisfied.

PINDARUS.

I do not doubt

But that my noble master will appear

Such as he is, full of regard and honour.

BRUTUS.

He is not doubted. A word, Lucilius;

How he received you, let me be resolv'd.

LUCILIUS.

With courtesy and with respect enough,

But not with such familiar instances,

Nor with such free and friendly conference,

As he hath us'd of old.

BRUTUS.

Thou hast describ'd

A hot friend cooling. Ever note, Lucilius,

When love begins to sicken and decay

It useth an enforced ceremony.

There are no tricks in plain and simple faith;

But hollow men, like horses hot at hand,

Make gallant show and promise of their mettle;

[Low march within.]

But when they should endure the bloody spur,

They fall their crests, and like deceitful jades

Sink in the trial. Comes his army on?

LUCILIUS.

They meant this night in Sardis to be quarter'd;

The greater part, the horse in general,

Are come with Cassius.

Enter Cassius and Soldiers.

BRUTUS.

Hark! he is arriv'd.

March gently on to meet him.

CASSIUS.

Stand, ho!

BRUTUS.

Stand, ho! Speak the word along.

FIRST SOLDIER.

Stand!

SECOND SOLDIER.

Stand!

THIRD SOLDIER.

Stand!

CASSIUS.

Most noble brother, you have done me wrong.

BRUTUS.

Judge me, you gods; wrong I mine enemies?

And if not so, how should I wrong a brother?

CASSIUS.

Brutus, this sober form of yours hides wrongs;

And when you do them—

BRUTUS.

Cassius, be content.

Speak your griefs softly, I do know you well.

Before the eyes of both our armies here,

Which should perceive nothing but love from us,

Let us not wrangle. Bid them move away;

Then in my tent, Cassius, enlarge your griefs,

And I will give you audience.

CASSIUS.

Pindarus,

Bid our commanders lead their charges off

A little from this ground.

BRUTUS.

Lucilius, do you the like; and let no man

Come to our tent till we have done our conference.

Lucius and Titinius, guard our door.

[Exeunt.]

SCENE III. Within the tent of Brutus.

Enter Brutus and Cassius.

CASSIUS.

That you have wrong'd me doth appear in this:

You have condemn'd and noted Lucius Pella

For taking bribes here of the Sardians;

Wherein my letters, praying on his side

Because I knew the man, were slighted off.

BRUTUS.

You wrong'd yourself to write in such a case.

CASSIUS.

In such a time as this it is not meet

That every nice offence should bear his comment.

BRUTUS.

Let me tell you, Cassius, you yourself

Are much condemn'd to have an itching palm,

To sell and mart your offices for gold

To undeservers.

CASSIUS.

I an itching palm!

You know that you are Brutus that speak this,

Or, by the gods, this speech were else your last.

BRUTUS.

The name of Cassius honours this corruption,

And chastisement doth therefore hide his head.

CASSIUS.

Chastisement!

BRUTUS.

Remember March, the Ides of March remember:

Did not great Julius bleed for justice' sake?

What villain touch'd his body, that did stab,

And not for justice? What! Shall one of us,

That struck the foremost man of all this world

But for supporting robbers, shall we now

Contaminate our fingers with base bribes,

And sell the mighty space of our large honours

For so much trash as may be grasped thus?

I had rather be a dog, and bay the moon,

Than such a Roman.

CASSIUS.

Brutus, bait not me,

I'll not endure it. You forget yourself,

To hedge me in. I am a soldier, I,

Older in practice, abler than yourself

To make conditions.

BRUTUS.

Go to; you are not, Cassius.

CASSIUS.

I am.

BRUTUS.

I say you are not.

CASSIUS.

Urge me no more, I shall forget myself;

Have mind upon your health, tempt me no farther.

BRUTUS.

Away, slight man!

CASSIUS.

Is't possible?

BRUTUS.

Hear me, for I will speak.

Must I give way and room to your rash choler?

Shall I be frighted when a madman stares?

CASSIUS.

O ye gods, ye gods! Must I endure all this?

BRUTUS.

All this? ay, more: fret till your proud heart break;

Go show your slaves how choleric you are,

And make your bondmen tremble. Must I budge?

Must I observe you? Must I stand and crouch

Under your testy humour? By the gods,

You shall digest the venom of your spleen,

Though it do split you; for, from this day forth,

I'll use you for my mirth, yea, for my laughter,

When you are waspish.

CASSIUS.

Is it come to this?

BRUTUS.

You say you are a better soldier:

Let it appear so; make your vaunting true,

And it shall please me well. For mine own part,

I shall be glad to learn of noble men.

CASSIUS.

You wrong me every way, you wrong me, Brutus.

I said, an elder soldier, not a better:

Did I say better?

BRUTUS.

If you did, I care not.

CASSIUS.

When Caesar liv'd, he durst not thus have mov'd me.

BRUTUS.

Peace, peace! you durst not so have tempted him.

CASSIUS.

I durst not?

BRUTUS.

No.

CASSIUS.

What? durst not tempt him?

BRUTUS.

For your life you durst not.

CASSIUS.

Do not presume too much upon my love.

I may do that I shall be sorry for.

BRUTUS.

You have done that you should be sorry for.

There is no terror, Cassius, in your threats,

For I am arm'd so strong in honesty,

That they pass by me as the idle wind,

Which I respect not. I did send to you

For certain sums of gold, which you denied me;

For I can raise no money by vile means:

By Heaven, I had rather coin my heart,

And drop my blood for drachmas, than to wring

From the hard hands of peasants their vile trash

By any indirection. I did send

To you for gold to pay my legions,

Which you denied me: was that done like Cassius?

Should I have answer'd Caius Cassius so?

When Marcus Brutus grows so covetous,

To lock such rascal counters from his friends,

Be ready, gods, with all your thunderbolts,

Dash him to pieces!

CASSIUS.

I denied you not.

BRUTUS.

You did.

CASSIUS.

I did not. He was but a fool

That brought my answer back. Brutus hath riv'd my heart.

A friend should bear his friend's infirmities;

But Brutus makes mine greater than they are.

BRUTUS.

I do not, till you practise them on me.

CASSIUS.

You love me not.

BRUTUS.

I do not like your faults.

CASSIUS.

A friendly eye could never see such faults.

BRUTUS.

A flatterer's would not, though they do appear

As huge as high Olympus.

CASSIUS.

Come, Antony, and young Octavius, come,

Revenge yourselves alone on Cassius,

For Cassius is a-weary of the world:

Hated by one he loves; brav'd by his brother;

Check'd like a bondman; all his faults observ'd,

Set in a note-book, learn'd and conn'd by rote,

To cast into my teeth. O, I could weep

My spirit from mine eyes! There is my dagger,

And here my naked breast; within, a heart

Dearer than Plutus' mine, richer than gold:

If that thou be'st a Roman, take it forth.

I, that denied thee gold, will give my heart:

Strike as thou didst at Caesar; for I know,

When thou didst hate him worst, thou lovedst him better

Than ever thou lovedst Cassius.

BRUTUS.

Sheathe your dagger.

Be angry when you will, it shall have scope;

Do what you will, dishonour shall be humour.

O Cassius, you are yoked with a lamb

That carries anger as the flint bears fire,

Who, much enforced, shows a hasty spark,

And straight is cold again.

CASSIUS.

Hath Cassius liv'd

To be but mirth and laughter to his Brutus,

When grief and blood ill-temper'd vexeth him?

BRUTUS.

When I spoke that, I was ill-temper'd too.

CASSIUS.

Do you confess so much? Give me your hand.

BRUTUS.

And my heart too.

CASSIUS.

O Brutus!

BRUTUS.

What's the matter?

CASSIUS.

Have not you love enough to bear with me,

When that rash humour which my mother gave me

Makes me forgetful?

BRUTUS.

Yes, Cassius; and from henceforth,

When you are over-earnest with your Brutus,

He'll think your mother chides, and leave you so.

Enter Poet, followed by Lucilius, Titinius and Lucius.

POET.

[Within.] Let me go in to see the generals,

There is some grudge between 'em; 'tis not meet

They be alone.

LUCILIUS.

[Within.] You shall not come to them.

POET.

[Within.] Nothing but death shall stay me.

CASSIUS.

How now! What's the matter?

POET.

For shame, you generals! What do you mean?

Love, and be friends, as two such men should be;

For I have seen more years, I'm sure, than ye.

CASSIUS.

Ha, ha! How vilely doth this cynic rhyme!

BRUTUS.

Get you hence, sirrah. Saucy fellow, hence!

CASSIUS.

Bear with him, Brutus; 'tis his fashion.

BRUTUS.

I'll know his humour when he knows his time.

What should the wars do with these jigging fools?

Companion, hence!

CASSIUS.

Away, away, be gone!

[Exit Poet.]

BRUTUS.

Lucilius and Titinius, bid the commanders

Prepare to lodge their companies tonight.

CASSIUS.

And come yourselves and bring Messala with you

Immediately to us.

[Exeunt Lucilius and Titinius.]

BRUTUS.

Lucius, a bowl of wine.

[Exit Lucius.]

CASSIUS.

I did not think you could have been so angry.

BRUTUS.

O Cassius, I am sick of many griefs.

CASSIUS.

Of your philosophy you make no use,

If you give place to accidental evils.

BRUTUS.

No man bears sorrow better. Portia is dead.

CASSIUS.

Ha? Portia?

BRUTUS.

She is dead.

CASSIUS.

How 'scap'd I killing, when I cross'd you so?

O insupportable and touching loss!

Upon what sickness?

BRUTUS.

Impatient of my absence,

And grief that young Octavius with Mark Antony

Have made themselves so strong; for with her death

That tidings came. With this she fell distract,

And, her attendants absent, swallow'd fire.

CASSIUS.

And died so?

BRUTUS.

Even so.

CASSIUS.

O ye immortal gods!

Enter Lucius, with wine and a taper.

BRUTUS.

Speak no more of her. Give me a bowl of wine.

In this I bury all unkindness, Cassius.

[Drinks.]

CASSIUS.

My heart is thirsty for that noble pledge.

Fill, Lucius, till the wine o'erswell the cup.

I cannot drink too much of Brutus' love.

[Drinks.]

[Exit Lucius.]

Enter Titinius and Messala.

BRUTUS.

Come in, Titinius!

Welcome, good Messala.

Now sit we close about this taper here,

And call in question our necessities.

CASSIUS.

Portia, art thou gone?

BRUTUS.

No more, I pray you.

Messala, I have here received letters,

That young Octavius and Mark Antony

Come down upon us with a mighty power,

Bending their expedition toward Philippi.

MESSALA.

Myself have letters of the selfsame tenor.

BRUTUS.

With what addition?

MESSALA.

That by proscription and bills of outlawry

Octavius, Antony, and Lepidus

Have put to death an hundred Senators.

BRUTUS.

Therein our letters do not well agree.

Mine speak of seventy Senators that died

By their proscriptions, Cicero being one.

CASSIUS.

Cicero one!

MESSALA.

Cicero is dead,

And by that order of proscription.

Had you your letters from your wife, my lord?

BRUTUS.

No, Messala.

MESSALA.

Nor nothing in your letters writ of her?

BRUTUS.

Nothing, Messala.

MESSALA.

That, methinks, is strange.

BRUTUS.

Why ask you? Hear you aught of her in yours?

MESSALA.

No, my lord.

BRUTUS.

Now as you are a Roman, tell me true.

MESSALA.

Then like a Roman bear the truth I tell,

For certain she is dead, and by strange manner.

BRUTUS.

Why, farewell, Portia. We must die, Messala.

With meditating that she must die once,

I have the patience to endure it now.

MESSALA.

Even so great men great losses should endure.

CASSIUS.

I have as much of this in art as you,

But yet my nature could not bear it so.

BRUTUS.

Well, to our work alive. What do you think

Of marching to Philippi presently?

CASSIUS.

I do not think it good.

BRUTUS.

Your reason?

CASSIUS.

This it is:

'Tis better that the enemy seek us;

So shall he waste his means, weary his soldiers,

Doing himself offence, whilst we, lying still,

Are full of rest, defence, and nimbleness.

BRUTUS.

Good reasons must of force give place to better.

The people 'twixt Philippi and this ground

Do stand but in a forced affection;

For they have grudg'd us contribution.

The enemy, marching along by them,

By them shall make a fuller number up,

Come on refresh'd, new-added, and encourag'd;

From which advantage shall we cut him off

If at Philippi we do face him there,

These people at our back.

CASSIUS.

Hear me, good brother.

BRUTUS.

Under your pardon. You must note besides,

That we have tried the utmost of our friends,

Our legions are brim-full, our cause is ripe.

The enemy increaseth every day;

We, at the height, are ready to decline.

There is a tide in the affairs of men,

Which, taken at the flood, leads on to fortune;

Omitted, all the voyage of their life

Is bound in shallows and in miseries.

On such a full sea are we now afloat,

And we must take the current when it serves,

Or lose our ventures.

CASSIUS.

Then, with your will, go on:

We'll along ourselves, and meet them at Philippi.

BRUTUS.

The deep of night is crept upon our talk,

And nature must obey necessity,

Which we will niggard with a little rest.

There is no more to say?

CASSIUS.

No more. Good night:

Early tomorrow will we rise, and hence.

Enter Lucius.

BRUTUS.

Lucius! My gown.

[Exit Lucius.]

Farewell now, good Messala.

Good night, Titinius. Noble, noble Cassius,

Good night, and good repose.

CASSIUS.

O my dear brother!

This was an ill beginning of the night.

Never come such division 'tween our souls!

Let it not, Brutus.

Enter Lucius with the gown.

BRUTUS.

Everything is well.

CASSIUS.

Good night, my lord.

BRUTUS.

Good night, good brother.

TITINIUS and MESSALA.

Good night, Lord Brutus.

BRUTUS.

Farewell, everyone.

[Exeunt Cassius, Titinius and Messala.]

Give me the gown. Where is thy instrument?

LUCIUS.

Here in the tent.

BRUTUS.

What, thou speak'st drowsily?

Poor knave, I blame thee not, thou art o'er-watch'd.

Call Claudius and some other of my men;

I'll have them sleep on cushions in my tent.

LUCIUS.

Varro and Claudius!

Enter Varro and Claudius.

VARRO.

Calls my lord?

BRUTUS.

I pray you, sirs, lie in my tent and sleep;

It may be I shall raise you by-and-by

On business to my brother Cassius.

VARRO.

So please you, we will stand and watch your pleasure.

BRUTUS.

I will not have it so; lie down, good sirs,

It may be I shall otherwise bethink me.

Look, Lucius, here's the book I sought for so;

I put it in the pocket of my gown.

[Servants lie down.]

LUCIUS.

I was sure your lordship did not give it me.

BRUTUS.

Bear with me, good boy, I am much forgetful.

Canst thou hold up thy heavy eyes awhile,

And touch thy instrument a strain or two?

LUCIUS.

Ay, my lord, an't please you.

BRUTUS.

It does, my boy.

I trouble thee too much, but thou art willing.

LUCIUS.

It is my duty, sir.

BRUTUS.

I should not urge thy duty past thy might;

I know young bloods look for a time of rest.

LUCIUS.

I have slept, my lord, already.

BRUTUS.

It was well done, and thou shalt sleep again;

I will not hold thee long. If I do live,

I will be good to thee.

[Lucius plays and sings till he falls asleep.]

This is a sleepy tune. O murd'rous slumber,

Layest thou thy leaden mace upon my boy,

That plays thee music? Gentle knave, good night;

I will not do thee so much wrong to wake thee.

If thou dost nod, thou break'st thy instrument;

I'll take it from thee; and, good boy, good night.

Let me see, let me see; is not the leaf turn'd down

Where I left reading? Here it is, I think.

Enter the Ghost of Caesar.

How ill this taper burns! Ha! who comes here?

I think it is the weakness of mine eyes

That shapes this monstrous apparition.

It comes upon me. Art thou anything?

Art thou some god, some angel, or some devil,

That mak'st my blood cold and my hair to stare?

Speak to me what thou art.

GHOST.

Thy evil spirit, Brutus.

BRUTUS.

Why com'st thou?

GHOST.

To tell thee thou shalt see me at Philippi.

BRUTUS.

141

Well; then I shall see thee again?

GHOST.

Ay, at Philippi.

BRUTUS.

Why, I will see thee at Philippi then.

[Ghost vanishes.]

Now I have taken heart, thou vanishest.

Ill spirit, I would hold more talk with thee.

Boy! Lucius! Varro! Claudius! Sirs, awake! Claudius!

LUCIUS.

The strings, my lord, are false.

BRUTUS.

He thinks he still is at his instrument.

Lucius, awake!

LUCIUS.

My lord?

BRUTUS.

Didst thou dream, Lucius, that thou so criedst out?

LUCIUS.

My lord, I do not know that I did cry.

BRUTUS.

Yes, that thou didst. Didst thou see anything?

LUCIUS.

Nothing, my lord.

BRUTUS.

Sleep again, Lucius. Sirrah Claudius!

Fellow thou, awake!

VARRO.

My lord?

CLAUDIUS.

My lord?

BRUTUS.

Why did you so cry out, sirs, in your sleep?

VARRO. CLAUDIUS.

Did we, my lord?

BRUTUS.

Ay. Saw you anything?

VARRO.

No, my lord, I saw nothing.

CLAUDIUS.

Nor I, my lord.

BRUTUS.

Go and commend me to my brother Cassius;

Bid him set on his powers betimes before,

And we will follow.

VARRO. CLAUDIUS.

It shall be done, my lord.

[Exeunt.]

143

ACT V

SCENE I. The plains of Philippi.

Enter Octavius, Antony and their Army.

OCTAVIUS.

Now, Antony, our hopes are answered.

You said the enemy would not come down,

But keep the hills and upper regions.

It proves not so; their battles are at hand,

They mean to warn us at Philippi here,

Answering before we do demand of them.

ANTONY.

Tut, I am in their bosoms, and I know

Wherefore they do it. They could be content

To visit other places, and come down

With fearful bravery, thinking by this face

To fasten in our thoughts that they have courage;

But 'tis not so.

Enter a Messenger.

MESSENGER.

Prepare you, generals.

The enemy comes on in gallant show;

Their bloody sign of battle is hung out,

And something to be done immediately.

ANTONY.

Octavius, lead your battle softly on

Upon the left hand of the even field.

OCTAVIUS.

Upon the right hand I. Keep thou the left.

ANTONY.

Why do you cross me in this exigent?

OCTAVIUS.

I do not cross you; but I will do so.

[March.]

Drum. Enter Brutus, Cassius and their Army; Lucilius, Titinius, Messala and others.

BRUTUS.

They stand, and would have parley.

CASSIUS.

Stand fast, Titinius; we must out and talk.

OCTAVIUS.

Mark Antony, shall we give sign of battle?

ANTONY.

No, Caesar, we will answer on their charge.

Make forth; the generals would have some words.

OCTAVIUS.

Stir not until the signal.

BRUTUS.

Words before blows: is it so, countrymen?

OCTAVIUS.

Not that we love words better, as you do.

BRUTUS.

Good words are better than bad strokes, Octavius.

ANTONY.

In your bad strokes, Brutus, you give good words;

Witness the hole you made in Caesar's heart,

Crying, "Long live! Hail, Caesar!"

CASSIUS.

Antony,

The posture of your blows are yet unknown;

But for your words, they rob the Hybla bees,

And leave them honeyless.

ANTONY.

Not stingless too.

BRUTUS.

O yes, and soundless too,

For you have stol'n their buzzing, Antony,

And very wisely threat before you sting.

ANTONY.

Villains, you did not so when your vile daggers

Hack'd one another in the sides of Caesar:

You show'd your teeth like apes, and fawn'd like hounds,

And bow'd like bondmen, kissing Caesar's feet;

Whilst damned Casca, like a cur, behind

Struck Caesar on the neck. O you flatterers!

CASSIUS.

Flatterers! Now, Brutus, thank yourself.

This tongue had not offended so today,

If Cassius might have rul'd.

OCTAVIUS.

Come, come, the cause. If arguing makes us sweat,

The proof of it will turn to redder drops.

Look, I draw a sword against conspirators.

When think you that the sword goes up again?

Never, till Caesar's three and thirty wounds

Be well aveng'd; or till another Caesar

Have added slaughter to the sword of traitors.

BRUTUS.

Caesar, thou canst not die by traitors' hands,

Unless thou bring'st them with thee.

OCTAVIUS.

So I hope.

I was not born to die on Brutus' sword.

BRUTUS.

O, if thou wert the noblest of thy strain,

Young man, thou couldst not die more honourable.

CASSIUS.

A peevish school-boy, worthless of such honour,

Join'd with a masker and a reveller.

ANTONY.

Old Cassius still!

OCTAVIUS.

Come, Antony; away!

Defiance, traitors, hurl we in your teeth.

If you dare fight today, come to the field;

If not, when you have stomachs.

[Exeunt Octavius, Antony and their Army.]

CASSIUS.

Why now, blow wind, swell billow, and swim bark!

The storm is up, and all is on the hazard.

BRUTUS.

Ho, Lucilius! Hark, a word with you.

LUCILIUS.

My lord?

[Brutus and Lucilius talk apart.]

CASSIUS.

Messala.

MESSALA.

What says my General?

CASSIUS.

Messala,

This is my birth-day; as this very day

Was Cassius born. Give me thy hand, Messala:

Be thou my witness that against my will

As Pompey was, am I compell'd to set

Upon one battle all our liberties.

You know that I held Epicurus strong,

And his opinion. Now I change my mind,

And partly credit things that do presage.

Coming from Sardis, on our former ensign

Two mighty eagles fell, and there they perch'd,

Gorging and feeding from our soldiers' hands,

Who to Philippi here consorted us.

This morning are they fled away and gone,

And in their steads do ravens, crows, and kites

Fly o'er our heads, and downward look on us,

As we were sickly prey: their shadows seem

A canopy most fatal, under which

Our army lies, ready to give up the ghost.

MESSALA.

Believe not so.

CASSIUS.

I but believe it partly,

For I am fresh of spirit, and resolv'd

To meet all perils very constantly.

BRUTUS.

Even so, Lucilius.

CASSIUS.

Now, most noble Brutus,

The gods today stand friendly, that we may,

Lovers in peace, lead on our days to age!

But, since the affairs of men rest still incertain,

Let's reason with the worst that may befall.

If we do lose this battle, then is this

The very last time we shall speak together:

What are you then determined to do?

BRUTUS.

Even by the rule of that philosophy

By which I did blame Cato for the death

Which he did give himself, I know not how,

But I do find it cowardly and vile,

For fear of what might fall, so to prevent

The time of life, arming myself with patience

To stay the providence of some high powers

That govern us below.

CASSIUS.

Then, if we lose this battle,

You are contented to be led in triumph

Thorough the streets of Rome?

BRUTUS.

No, Cassius, no: think not, thou noble Roman,

That ever Brutus will go bound to Rome;

He bears too great a mind. But this same day

Must end that work the Ides of March begun;

And whether we shall meet again I know not.

Therefore our everlasting farewell take.

For ever, and for ever, farewell, Cassius.

If we do meet again, why, we shall smile;

If not, why then this parting was well made.

CASSIUS.

For ever and for ever farewell, Brutus.

If we do meet again, we'll smile indeed;

If not, 'tis true this parting was well made.

BRUTUS.

Why then, lead on. O, that a man might know

The end of this day's business ere it come!

But it sufficeth that the day will end,

And then the end is known. Come, ho! away!

[Exeunt.]

SCENE II. The same. The field of battle.

Alarum. Enter Brutus and Messala.

BRUTUS.

Ride, ride, Messala, ride, and give these bills

Unto the legions on the other side.

[Loud alarum.]

Let them set on at once; for I perceive

But cold demeanor in Octavius' wing,

And sudden push gives them the overthrow.

Ride, ride, Messala; let them all come down.

[Exeunt.]

SCENE III. Another part of the field.

Alarum. Enter Cassius and Titinius.

CASSIUS.

O, look, Titinius, look, the villains fly!

Myself have to mine own turn'd enemy:

This ensign here of mine was turning back;

I slew the coward, and did take it from him.

TITINIUS.

O Cassius, Brutus gave the word too early,

Who, having some advantage on Octavius,

Took it too eagerly: his soldiers fell to spoil,

Whilst we by Antony are all enclos'd.

Enter Pindarus.

PINDARUS.

Fly further off, my lord, fly further off;

Mark Antony is in your tents, my lord.

Fly, therefore, noble Cassius, fly far off.

CASSIUS.

This hill is far enough. Look, look, Titinius;

Are those my tents where I perceive the fire?

TITINIUS.

They are, my lord.

CASSIUS.

Titinius, if thou lovest me,

Mount thou my horse and hide thy spurs in him,

Till he have brought thee up to yonder troops

And here again, that I may rest assur'd

Whether yond troops are friend or enemy.

TITINIUS.

I will be here again, even with a thought.

[Exit.]

CASSIUS.

Go, Pindarus, get higher on that hill,

My sight was ever thick. Regard Titinius,

And tell me what thou notest about the field.

[Pindarus goes up.]

This day I breathed first. Time is come round,

And where I did begin, there shall I end.

My life is run his compass. Sirrah, what news?

PINDARUS.

[Above.] O my lord!

CASSIUS.

What news?

PINDARUS.

[Above.] Titinius is enclosed round about

With horsemen, that make to him on the spur,

Yet he spurs on. Now they are almost on him.

Now, Titinius! Now some light. O, he lights too.

He's ta'en!

[Shout.]

And, hark! they shout for joy.

CASSIUS.

Come down; behold no more.

O, coward that I am, to live so long,

To see my best friend ta'en before my face!

[Pindarus descends.]

Come hither, sirrah.

In Parthia did I take thee prisoner;

And then I swore thee, saving of thy life,

That whatsoever I did bid thee do,

Thou shouldst attempt it. Come now, keep thine oath.

Now be a freeman; and with this good sword,

That ran through Caesar's bowels, search this bosom.

Stand not to answer. Here, take thou the hilts;

And when my face is cover'd, as 'tis now,

Guide thou the sword.—Caesar, thou art reveng'd,

Even with the sword that kill'd thee.

[Dies.]

PINDARUS.

So, I am free, yet would not so have been,

Durst I have done my will. O Cassius!

Far from this country Pindarus shall run,

Where never Roman shall take note of him.

[Exit.]

Enter Titinius with Messala.

MESSALA.

It is but change, Titinius; for Octavius

Is overthrown by noble Brutus' power,

As Cassius' legions are by Antony.

TITINIUS.

These tidings would well comfort Cassius.

MESSALA.

Where did you leave him?

TITINIUS.

All disconsolate,

With Pindarus his bondman, on this hill.

MESSALA.

Is not that he that lies upon the ground?

TITINIUS.

He lies not like the living. O my heart!

MESSALA.

Is not that he?

TITINIUS.

No, this was he, Messala,

But Cassius is no more. O setting sun,

As in thy red rays thou dost sink to night,

So in his red blood Cassius' day is set.

The sun of Rome is set. Our day is gone;

Clouds, dews, and dangers come; our deeds are done.

Mistrust of my success hath done this deed.

MESSALA.

Mistrust of good success hath done this deed.

O hateful Error, Melancholy's child!

Why dost thou show to the apt thoughts of men

The things that are not? O Error, soon conceiv'd,

Thou never com'st unto a happy birth,

But kill'st the mother that engender'd thee!

TITINIUS.

What, Pindarus! where art thou, Pindarus?

MESSALA.

Seek him, Titinius, whilst I go to meet

The noble Brutus, thrusting this report

Into his ears. I may say thrusting it;

For piercing steel and darts envenomed

Shall be as welcome to the ears of Brutus

As tidings of this sight.

TITINIUS.

Hie you, Messala,

And I will seek for Pindarus the while.

[Exit Messala.]

Why didst thou send me forth, brave Cassius?

Did I not meet thy friends? And did not they

Put on my brows this wreath of victory,

And bid me give it thee? Didst thou not hear their shouts?

Alas, thou hast misconstrued everything!

But, hold thee, take this garland on thy brow;

Thy Brutus bid me give it thee, and I

Will do his bidding. Brutus, come apace,

And see how I regarded Caius Cassius.

By your leave, gods. This is a Roman's part.

Come, Cassius' sword, and find Titinius' heart.

[Dies.]

Alarum. Enter Brutus, Messala, young Cato, Strato, Volumnius and Lucilius.

BRUTUS.

Where, where, Messala, doth his body lie?

MESSALA.

Lo, yonder, and Titinius mourning it.

BRUTUS.

Titinius' face is upward.

CATO.

He is slain.

BRUTUS.

O Julius Caesar, thou art mighty yet!

Thy spirit walks abroad, and turns our swords

In our own proper entrails.

[Low alarums.]

CATO.

Brave Titinius!

Look whether he have not crown'd dead Cassius!

BRUTUS.

Are yet two Romans living such as these?

The last of all the Romans, fare thee well!

It is impossible that ever Rome

Should breed thy fellow. Friends, I owe more tears

To this dead man than you shall see me pay.

I shall find time, Cassius, I shall find time.

Come therefore, and to Thassos send his body.

His funerals shall not be in our camp,

Lest it discomfort us. Lucilius, come;

And come, young Cato; let us to the field.

Labeo and Flavius, set our battles on.

'Tis three o'clock; and Romans, yet ere night

We shall try fortune in a second fight.

[Exeunt.]

SCENE IV. Another part of the field.

Alarum. Enter fighting soldiers of both armies; then Brutus, Messala, young Cato, Lucilius, Flavius and others.

BRUTUS.

Yet, countrymen, O, yet hold up your heads!

CATO.

What bastard doth not? Who will go with me?

I will proclaim my name about the field.

I am the son of Marcus Cato, ho!

A foe to tyrants, and my country's friend.

I am the son of Marcus Cato, ho!

[Charges the enemy.]

LUCILIUS.

And I am Brutus, Marcus Brutus, I;

Brutus, my country's friend; know me for Brutus!

[Exit, charging the enemy. Cato is overpowered, and falls.]

LUCILIUS.

O young and noble Cato, art thou down?

Why, now thou diest as bravely as Titinius,

And mayst be honour'd, being Cato's son.

FIRST SOLDIER.

Yield, or thou diest.

LUCILIUS.

Only I yield to die:

There is so much that thou wilt kill me straight;

[Offering money]

Kill Brutus, and be honour'd in his death.

FIRST SOLDIER.

We must not. A noble prisoner!

SECOND SOLDIER.

Room, ho! Tell Antony, Brutus is ta'en.

FIRST SOLDIER.

I'll tell the news. Here comes the General.

Enter Antony.

Brutus is ta'en, Brutus is ta'en, my lord.

ANTONY.

Where is he?

LUCILIUS.

Safe, Antony; Brutus is safe enough.

I dare assure thee that no enemy

Shall ever take alive the noble Brutus.

The gods defend him from so great a shame!

When you do find him, or alive or dead,

He will be found like Brutus, like himself.

ANTONY.

This is not Brutus, friend; but, I assure you,

A prize no less in worth. Keep this man safe,

Give him all kindness. I had rather have

Such men my friends than enemies. Go on,

And see whether Brutus be alive or dead;

And bring us word unto Octavius' tent

How everything is chanc'd.

                                  [Exeunt.]

SCENE V. Another part of the field.

Enter Brutus, Dardanius, Clitus, Strato and Volumnius.

BRUTUS.

Come, poor remains of friends, rest on this rock.

CLITUS.

Statilius show'd the torch-light; but, my lord,

He came not back: he is or ta'en or slain.

BRUTUS.

Sit thee down, Clitus. Slaying is the word;

It is a deed in fashion. Hark thee, Clitus.

[Whispering.]

CLITUS.

What, I, my lord? No, not for all the world.

BRUTUS.

Peace then, no words.

CLITUS.

I'll rather kill myself.

BRUTUS.

Hark thee, Dardanius.

[Whispers him.]

DARDANIUS.

Shall I do such a deed?

CLITUS.

O Dardanius!

DARDANIUS.

O Clitus!

CLITUS.

What ill request did Brutus make to thee?

DARDANIUS.

To kill him, Clitus. Look, he meditates.

CLITUS.

Now is that noble vessel full of grief,

That it runs over even at his eyes.

BRUTUS.

Come hither, good Volumnius; list a word.

VOLUMNIUS.

What says my lord?

BRUTUS.

Why, this, Volumnius:

The ghost of Caesar hath appear'd to me

Two several times by night; at Sardis once,

And this last night here in Philippi fields.

I know my hour is come.

VOLUMNIUS.

Not so, my lord.

BRUTUS.

Nay I am sure it is, Volumnius.

Thou seest the world, Volumnius, how it goes;

Our enemies have beat us to the pit.

[Low alarums.]

It is more worthy to leap in ourselves

Than tarry till they push us. Good Volumnius,

Thou know'st that we two went to school together;

Even for that our love of old, I pr'ythee

Hold thou my sword-hilts, whilst I run on it.

VOLUMNIUS.

That's not an office for a friend, my lord.

[Alarums still.]

CLITUS.

Fly, fly, my lord! there is no tarrying here.

BRUTUS.

Farewell to you; and you; and you, Volumnius.

Strato, thou hast been all this while asleep;

Farewell to thee too, Strato.—Countrymen,

My heart doth joy, that yet in all my life

I found no man but he was true to me.

I shall have glory by this losing day

More than Octavius and Mark Antony

By this vile conquest shall attain unto.

So fare you well at once; for Brutus' tongue

Hath almost ended his life's history.

Night hangs upon mine eyes; my bones would rest,

That have but labour'd to attain this hour.

> [Alarums. Cry within, "Fly, fly, fly!".]

CLITUS.

Fly, my lord, fly!

BRUTUS.

Hence! I will follow.

> [Exeunt Clitus, Dardanius and Volumnius.]

I pr'ythee, Strato, stay thou by thy lord.

Thou art a fellow of a good respect;

Thy life hath had some smatch of honour in it.

Hold then my sword, and turn away thy face,

While I do run upon it. Wilt thou, Strato?

STRATO.

Give me your hand first. Fare you well, my lord.

BRUTUS.

Farewell, good Strato.—Caesar, now be still:

I kill'd not thee with half so good a will.

> [He runs on his sword, and dies.]

Alarum. Retreat. Enter Antony, Octavius, Messala, Lucilius and the Army.

OCTAVIUS.

What man is that?

MESSALA.

My master's man. Strato, where is thy master?

STRATO.

Free from the bondage you are in, Messala.

The conquerors can but make a fire of him;

For Brutus only overcame himself,

And no man else hath honour by his death.

LUCILIUS.

So Brutus should be found. I thank thee, Brutus,

That thou hast prov'd Lucilius' saying true.

OCTAVIUS.

All that serv'd Brutus, I will entertain them.

Fellow, wilt thou bestow thy time with me?

STRATO.

Ay, if Messala will prefer me to you.

OCTAVIUS.

Do so, good Messala.

MESSALA.

How died my master, Strato?

STRATO.

I held the sword, and he did run on it.

MESSALA.

Octavius, then take him to follow thee,

That did the latest service to my master.

ANTONY.

This was the noblest Roman of them all.

All the conspirators save only he,

Did that they did in envy of great Caesar;

He only, in a general honest thought

And common good to all, made one of them.

His life was gentle, and the elements

So mix'd in him that Nature might stand up

And say to all the world, "This was a man!"

OCTAVIUS.

According to his virtue let us use him

With all respect and rites of burial.

Within my tent his bones tonight shall lie,

Most like a soldier, order'd honourably.

So call the field to rest, and let's away,

To part the glories of this happy day.

[Exeunt.]

About Author

Shakespeare produced most of his known works between 1589 and 1613. His early plays were primarily comedies and histories and are regarded as some of the best work produced in these genres. Until about 1608, he wrote mainly tragedies, among them Hamlet, Othello, King Lear, and Macbeth, all considered to be among the finest works in the English language. In the last phase of his life, he wrote tragicomedies (also known as romances) and collaborated with other playwrights.

Many of Shakespeare's plays were published in editions of varying quality and accuracy in his lifetime. However, in 1623, two fellow actors and friends of Shakespeare's, John Heminges and Henry Condell, published a more definitive text known as the First Folio, a posthumous collected edition of Shakespeare's dramatic works that included all but two of his plays. The volume was prefaced with a poem by Ben Jonson, in which Jonson presciently hails Shakespeare in a now-famous quote as "not of an age, but for all time".

Throughout the 20th and 21st centuries, Shakespeare's works have been continually adapted and rediscovered by new movements in scholarship and performance. His plays remain popular and are studied, performed, and reinterpreted through various cultural and political contexts around the world.

Early life

William Shakespeare was the son of John Shakespeare, an alderman and a successful glover (glove-maker) originally from Snitterfield, and Mary Arden, the daughter of an affluent landowning farmer. He was born in Stratford-upon-Avon and baptised there on 26 April 1564. His actual date of birth remains unknown, but is traditionally observed on 23 April, Saint George's Day. This date, which can be traced to a mistake made by an 18th-century scholar, has proved appealing to biographers because Shakespeare died on the same date in 1616. He was the third of eight children, and the eldest surviving son.

Although no attendance records for the period survive, most biographers agree that Shakespeare was probably educated at the King's New School in Stratford, a free school chartered in 1553, about a quarter-mile (400 m) from his home. Grammar schools varied in quality during the Elizabethan era, but grammar school curricula were largely similar: the basic Latin text was standardised by royal decree, and the school would have provided an intensive education in grammar based upon Latin classical authors.

At the age of 18, Shakespeare married 26-year-old Anne Hathaway. The consistory court of the Diocese of Worcester issued a marriage licence on 27 November 1582. The next day, two of Hathaway's neighbours posted bonds guaranteeing that no lawful claims impeded the marriage. The ceremony may have been arranged in some haste since the Worcester chancellor allowed the marriage banns to be read once instead of the usual three times, and six months after the marriage Anne gave birth to a daughter, Susanna, baptised 26 May 1583. Twins, son Hamnet and daughter Judith, followed almost two years later and were baptised 2 February 1585. Hamnet died of unknown causes at the age of 11 and was buried 11 August 1596.

After the birth of the twins, Shakespeare left few historical traces until he is mentioned as part of the London theatre scene in 1592. The exception is the appearance of his name in the "complaints bill" of a law case before the Queen's Bench court at Westminster dated Michaelmas Term 1588 and 9 October 1589. Scholars refer to the years between 1585 and 1592 as Shakespeare's "lost years". Biographers attempting to account for this period have reported many apocryphal stories. Nicholas Rowe, Shakespeare's first biographer, recounted a Stratford legend that Shakespeare fled the town for London to escape prosecution for deer poaching in the estate of local squire Thomas Lucy. Shakespeare is also supposed to have taken his revenge on Lucy by writing a scurrilous ballad about him. Another 18th-century story has Shakespeare starting his theatrical career minding the horses of theatre patrons in London. John Aubrey reported that Shakespeare had been a country schoolmaster. Some 20th-century scholars have suggested that Shakespeare may have been employed as a schoolmaster by Alexander

Hoghton of Lancashire, a Catholic landowner who named a certain "William Shakeshafte" in his will. Little evidence substantiates such stories other than hearsay collected after his death, and Shakeshafte was a common name in the Lancashire area.

London and theatrical career

It is not known definitively when Shakespeare began writing, but contemporary allusions and records of performances show that several of his plays were on the London stage by 1592. By then, he was sufficiently known in London to be attacked in print by the playwright Robert Greene in his Groats-Worth of Wit:

... there is an upstart Crow, beautified with our feathers, that with his Tiger's heart wrapped in a Player's hide, supposes he is as well able to bombast out a blank verse as the best of you: and being an absolute Johannes factotum, is in his own conceit the only Shake-scene in a country.

Scholars differ on the exact meaning of Greene's words, but most agree that Greene was accusing Shakespeare of reaching above his rank in trying to match such university-educated writers as Christopher Marlowe, Thomas Nashe, and Greene himself (the so-called "University Wits"). The italicised phrase parodying the line "Oh, tiger's heart wrapped in a woman's hide" from Shakespeare's Henry VI, Part 3, along with the pun "Shake-scene", clearly identify Shakespeare as Greene's target. As used here, Johannes Factotum ("Jack of all trades") refers to a second-rate tinkerer with the work of others, rather than the more common "universal genius".

Greene's attack is the earliest surviving mention of Shakespeare's work in the theatre. Biographers suggest that his career may have begun any time from the mid-1580s to just before Greene's remarks. After 1594, Shakespeare's plays were performed only by the Lord Chamberlain's Men, a company owned by a group of players, including Shakespeare, that soon became the leading playing company in London. After the death of Queen Elizabeth in 1603, the company was awarded a royal patent by the new King James I, and changed its name to the King's Men.

"All the world's a stage,

and all the men and women merely players:

they have their exits and their entrances;

and one man in his time plays many parts ..."

—As You Like It, Act II, Scene 7, 139–142

In 1599, a partnership of members of the company built their own theatre on the south bank of the River Thames, which they named the Globe. In 1608, the partnership also took over the Blackfriars indoor theatre. Extant records of Shakespeare's property purchases and investments indicate that his association with the company made him a wealthy man, and in 1597, he bought the second-largest house in Stratford, New Place, and in 1605, invested in a share of the parish tithes in Stratford.

Some of Shakespeare's plays were published in quarto editions, beginning in 1594, and by 1598, his name had become a selling point and began to appear on the title pages. Shakespeare continued to act in his own and other plays after his success as a playwright. The 1616 edition of Ben Jonson's Works names him on the cast lists for Every Man in His Humour (1598) and Sejanus His Fall (1603). The absence of his name from the 1605 cast list for Jonson's Volpone is taken by some scholars as a sign that his acting career was nearing its end. The First Folio of 1623, however, lists Shakespeare as one of "the Principal Actors in all these Plays", some of which were first staged after Volpone, although we cannot know for certain which roles he played. In 1610, John Davies of Hereford wrote that "good Will" played "kingly" roles. In 1709, Rowe passed down a tradition that Shakespeare played the ghost of Hamlet's father. Later traditions maintain that he also played Adam in As You Like It, and the Chorus in Henry V, though scholars doubt the sources of that information.

Throughout his career, Shakespeare divided his time between London and Stratford. In 1596, the year before he bought New Place as his family home in Stratford, Shakespeare was living in the parish of St. Helen's, Bishopsgate, north of the River Thames. He moved across the river to Southwark by 1599, the same year his company constructed the Globe Theatre there. By 1604, he had moved north of the river again, to an area north of St Paul's Cathedral with many fine houses. There, he rented rooms from a French Huguenot named Christopher Mountjoy, a maker of ladies' wigs and other headgear.

Later years and death

Rowe was the first biographer to record the tradition, repeated by Johnson, that Shakespeare retired to Stratford "some years before his death". He was still working as an actor in London in 1608; in an answer to the sharers' petition in 1635, Cuthbert Burbage stated that after purchasing the lease of the Blackfriars Theatre in 1608 from Henry Evans, the King's Men "placed men players" there, "which were Heminges, Condell, Shakespeare, etc.". However, it is perhaps relevant that the bubonic plague raged in London throughout 1609. The London public playhouses were repeatedly closed during extended outbreaks of the plague (a total of over 60 months closure between May 1603 and February 1610), which meant there was often no acting work. Retirement from all work was uncommon at that time. Shakespeare continued to visit London during the years 1611–1614. In 1612, he was called as a witness in Bellott v. Mountjoy, a court case concerning the marriage settlement of Mountjoy's daughter, Mary. In March 1613, he bought a gatehouse in the former Blackfriars priory; and from November 1614, he was in London for several weeks with his son-in-law, John Hall. After 1610, Shakespeare wrote fewer plays, and none are attributed to him after 1613. His last three plays were collaborations, probably with John Fletcher, who succeeded him as the house playwright of the King's Men.

Shakespeare died on 23 April 1616, at the age of 52. He died within a month of signing his will, a document which he begins by describing himself as being in "perfect health". No extant contemporary source explains how or why he died. Half a century later, John Ward, the vicar of Stratford, wrote in his notebook: "Shakespeare, Drayton, and Ben Jonson had a merry meeting and, it seems, drank too hard, for Shakespeare died of a fever there contracted", not an impossible scenario since Shakespeare knew Jonson and Drayton. Of the tributes from fellow authors, one refers to his relatively sudden death: "We wondered, Shakespeare, that thou went'st so soon / From the world's stage to the grave's tiring room."

He was survived by his wife and two daughters. Susanna had married a physician, John Hall, in 1607, and Judith had married Thomas Quiney, a vintner, two months before Shakespeare's death. Shakespeare signed his last will and testament on 25 March 1616; the following day, his new son-in-law, Thomas Quiney was found guilty of fathering an illegitimate son by Margaret Wheeler, who had died during childbirth. Thomas was ordered by the church court to do public penance, which would have caused much shame and embarrassment for the Shakespeare family.

Shakespeare bequeathed the bulk of his large estate to his elder daughter Susanna under stipulations that she pass it down intact to "the first son of her body". The Quineys had three children, all of whom died without marrying. The Halls had one child, Elizabeth, who married twice but died without children in 1670, ending Shakespeare's direct line. Shakespeare's will scarcely mentions his wife, Anne, who was probably entitled to one-third of his estate automatically. He did make a point, however, of leaving her "my second best bed", a bequest that has led to much speculation. Some scholars see the bequest as an insult to Anne, whereas others believe that the second-best bed would have been the matrimonial bed and therefore rich in significance.

Shakespeare was buried in the chancel of the Holy Trinity Church two days after his death. The epitaph carved into the stone slab covering his grave includes a curse against moving his bones, which was carefully avoided during restoration of the church in 2008:

Good frend for Iesvs sake forbeare,

To digg the dvst encloased heare.

Bleste be Middle English the.svg man Middle English that.svg spares thes stones,

And cvrst be he Middle English that.svg moves my bones.

(Modern spelling: Good friend, for Jesus' sake forbear, / To dig the dust enclosed here. / Blessed be the man that spares these stones, / And cursed be he that moves my bones.)

Some time before 1623, a funerary monument was erected in his memory on the north wall, with a half-effigy of him in the act of writing. Its plaque compares him to Nestor, Socrates, and Virgil. In 1623, in conjunction with the publication of the First Folio, the Droeshout engraving was published.

Shakespeare has been commemorated in many statues and memorials around the world, including funeral monuments in Southwark Cathedral and Poets' Corner in Westminster Abbey.

Plays

Most playwrights of the period typically collaborated with others at some point, and critics agree that Shakespeare did the same, mostly early and late in his career. Some attributions, such as Titus Andronicus and the early history plays, remain controversial while The Two Noble Kinsmen and the lost Cardenio have well-attested contemporary documentation. Textual evidence also supports the view that several of the plays were revised by other writers after their original composition.

The first recorded works of Shakespeare are Richard III and the three parts of Henry VI, written in the early 1590s during a vogue for historical drama. Shakespeare's plays are difficult to date precisely, however, and studies of the texts suggest that Titus Andronicus, The Comedy of Errors, The Taming of the Shrew, and The Two Gentlemen of Verona may also belong to Shakespeare's earliest period. His first histories, which draw heavily on the 1587 edition of Raphael Holinshed's Chronicles of England, Scotland, and Ireland, dramatise the destructive results of weak or corrupt rule and have been interpreted as a justification for the origins of the Tudor dynasty. The early plays were influenced by the works of other Elizabethan dramatists, especially Thomas Kyd and Christopher Marlowe, by the traditions of medieval drama, and by the plays of Seneca. The Comedy of Errors was also based on classical models, but no source for The Taming of the Shrew has been found, though it is related to a separate play of the same name and may have derived from a folk story. Like The Two Gentlemen of Verona, in which two friends appear to approve of rape, the Shrew's story of the taming of a woman's independent spirit by a man sometimes troubles modern critics, directors, and audiences.

Shakespeare's early classical and Italianate comedies, containing tight double plots and precise comic sequences, give way in the mid-1590s to the romantic atmosphere of his most acclaimed comedies. A Midsummer Night's Dream is a witty mixture of romance, fairy magic, and comic lowlife scenes. Shakespeare's next comedy, the equally romantic Merchant of Venice, contains a portrayal of the vengeful Jewish moneylender Shylock, which reflects Elizabethan views but may appear derogatory to modern audiences. The wit and wordplay of Much Ado About Nothing, the charming rural setting of As You Like It, and the lively merrymaking of Twelfth Night complete Shakespeare's sequence of great comedies. After the lyrical Richard II, written almost entirely in verse, Shakespeare introduced prose comedy into the histories of the late 1590s, Henry IV, parts 1 and 2, and Henry V. His characters become more complex and tender as he switches deftly between comic and serious scenes, prose and poetry, and achieves the narrative variety of his mature work. This period begins and ends with two tragedies: Romeo and Juliet, the famous romantic tragedy of sexually charged adolescence, love, and death; and Julius Caesar—based on Sir Thomas North's 1579 translation of Plutarch's Parallel Lives—which introduced a new kind of drama. According to Shakespearean scholar James Shapiro, in Julius Caesar, "the various strands of politics, character, inwardness, contemporary events, even Shakespeare's own reflections on the act of writing, began to infuse each other".

In the early 17th century, Shakespeare wrote the so-called "problem plays" Measure for Measure, Troilus and Cressida, and All's Well That Ends Well and a number of his best known tragedies. Many critics believe that Shakespeare's greatest tragedies represent the peak of his art. The titular hero of one of Shakespeare's greatest tragedies, Hamlet, has probably been discussed more than any other Shakespearean character, especially for his famous soliloquy which begins "To be or not to be; that is the question". Unlike the introverted Hamlet, whose fatal flaw is hesitation, the heroes of the tragedies that followed, Othello and King Lear, are undone by hasty errors of judgement. The plots of Shakespeare's tragedies often hinge on such fatal errors or flaws, which overturn order and destroy the hero and those he loves. In Othello, the villain Iago stokes Othello's sexual jealousy to the point where he murders the innocent wife who loves him. In King Lear, the old king commits the tragic error of giving up his powers, initiating the events which lead to the torture and blinding of the Earl of Gloucester and the murder of Lear's youngest daughter Cordelia. According to the critic Frank Kermode, "the play-offers neither its good characters nor its audience any relief from its cruelty". In Macbeth, the shortest and most compressed of Shakespeare's tragedies, uncontrollable ambition incites Macbeth and his wife, Lady Macbeth, to murder the rightful king and usurp the throne until their own guilt destroys them in turn. In this play, Shakespeare adds a supernatural element to the tragic structure. His last major tragedies, Antony and Cleopatra and Coriolanus, contain some of Shakespeare's finest poetry and were considered his most successful tragedies by the poet and critic T.S. Eliot.

In his final period, Shakespeare turned to romance or tragicomedy and completed three more major plays: Cymbeline, The Winter's Tale, and The Tempest, as well as the collaboration, Pericles, Prince of Tyre. Less bleak than the tragedies, these four plays are graver in tone than the comedies of the 1590s, but they end with reconciliation and the forgiveness of potentially tragic errors. Some commentators have seen this change in mood as evidence of a more serene view of life on Shakespeare's part, but it may merely reflect the theatrical fashion of the day. Shakespeare collaborated on two further surviving plays, Henry VIII and The Two Noble Kinsmen, probably with John Fletcher.

Performances

It is not clear for which companies Shakespeare wrote his early plays. The title page of the 1594 edition of Titus Andronicus reveals that the play had been acted by three different troupes. After the plagues of 1592–3, Shakespeare's plays were performed by his own company at The Theatre and the Curtain in Shoreditch, north of the Thames. Londoners flocked there to see the first part of Henry IV, Leonard Digges recording, "Let but Falstaff come, Hal, Poins, the rest ... and you scarce shall have a room". When the company found themselves in dispute with their landlord, they pulled The

Theatre down and used the timbers to construct the Globe Theatre, the first playhouse built by actors for actors, on the south bank of the Thames at Southwark. The Globe opened in autumn 1599, with Julius Caesar one of the first plays staged. Most of Shakespeare's greatest post-1599 plays were written for the Globe, including Hamlet, Othello, and King Lear.

After the Lord Chamberlain's Men were renamed the King's Men in 1603, they entered a special relationship with the new King James. Although the performance records are patchy, the King's Men performed seven of Shakespeare's plays at court between 1 November 1604, and 31 October 1605, including two performances of The Merchant of Venice. After 1608, they performed at the indoor Blackfriars Theatre during the winter and the Globe during the summer. The indoor setting, combined with the Jacobean fashion for lavishly staged masques, allowed Shakespeare to introduce more elaborate stage devices. In Cymbeline, for example, Jupiter descends "in thunder and lightning, sitting upon an eagle: he throws a thunderbolt. The ghosts fall on their knees."

The actors in Shakespeare's company included the famous Richard Burbage, William Kempe, Henry Condell and John Heminges. Burbage played the leading role in the first performances of many of Shakespeare's plays, including Richard III, Hamlet, Othello, and King Lear. The popular comic actor Will Kempe played the servant Peter in Romeo and Juliet and Dogberry in Much Ado About Nothing, among other characters. He was replaced around 1600 by Robert Armin, who played roles such as Touchstone in As You Like It and the fool in King Lear. In 1613, Sir Henry Wotton recorded that Henry VIII "was set forth with many extraordinary circumstances of pomp and ceremony". On 29 June, however, a cannon set fire to the thatch of the Globe and burned the theatre to the ground, an event which pinpoints the date of a Shakespeare play with rare precision.

Textual sources

In 1623, John Heminges and Henry Condell, two of Shakespeare's friends from the King's Men, published the First Folio, a collected edition of Shakespeare's plays. It contained 36 texts, including 18 printed for the

180

first time. Many of the plays had already appeared in quarto versions—flimsy books made from sheets of paper folded twice to make four leaves. No evidence suggests that Shakespeare approved these editions, which the First Folio describes as "stol'n and surreptitious copies". Nor did Shakespeare plan or expect his works to survive in any form at all; those works likely would have faded into oblivion but for his friends' spontaneous idea, after his death, to create and publish the First Folio.

Alfred Pollard termed some of the pre-1623 versions as "bad quartos" because of their adapted, paraphrased or garbled texts, which may in places have been reconstructed from memory. Where several versions of a play survive, each differs from the other. The differences may stem from copying or printing errors, from notes by actors or audience members, or from Shakespeare's own papers. In some cases, for example, Hamlet, Troilus and Cressida, and Othello, Shakespeare could have revised the texts between the quarto and folio editions. In the case of King Lear, however, while most modern editions do conflate them, the 1623 folio version is so different from the 1608 quarto that the Oxford Shakespeare prints them both, arguing that they cannot be conflated without confusion.

Influence from neighbours in London

Ten years of research by Geoffrey Marsh (museum director) of the Victoria and Albert Museum in London may have shown that Shakespeare got many of the ideas and information for his plays, from his neighbours that he lived near in London in the late 1590s.

Geoffrey Marsh found the site of Shakespeare's house in St Helen's Church, Bishopsgate parish, at the corner of St.Helen's churchyard and Bishopsgate Street, north of the churchyard, from the records of the Leathersellers Company. Many wealthy and notable people (including Sir John Spencer and Dr. Edward Jorden and Dr. Peter Turner), with connections across Europe, lived near Shakespeare.

Poems

In 1593 and 1594, when the theatres were closed because of plague,

Shakespeare published two narrative poems on sexual themes, Venus and Adonis and The Rape of Lucrece. He dedicated them to Henry Wriothesley, Earl of Southampton. In Venus and Adonis, an innocent Adonis rejects the sexual advances of Venus; while in The Rape of Lucrece, the virtuous wife Lucrece is raped by the lustful Tarquin. Influenced by Ovid's Metamorphoses, the poems show the guilt and moral confusion that result from uncontrolled lust. Both proved popular and were often reprinted during Shakespeare's lifetime. A third narrative poem, A Lover's Complaint, in which a young woman laments her seduction by a persuasive suitor, was printed in the first edition of the Sonnets in 1609. Most scholars now accept that Shakespeare wrote A Lover's Complaint. Critics consider that its fine qualities are marred by leaden effects. The Phoenix and the Turtle, printed in Robert Chester's 1601 Love's Martyr, mourns the deaths of the legendary phoenix and his lover, the faithful turtle dove. In 1599, two early drafts of sonnets 138 and 144 appeared in The Passionate Pilgrim, published under Shakespeare's name but without his permission.

Sonnets

Published in 1609, the Sonnets were the last of Shakespeare's non-dramatic works to be printed. Scholars are not certain when each of the 154 sonnets was composed, but evidence suggests that Shakespeare wrote sonnets throughout his career for a private readership. Even before the two unauthorised sonnets appeared in The Passionate Pilgrim in 1599, Francis Meres had referred in 1598 to Shakespeare's "sugred Sonnets among his private friends". Few analysts believe that the published collection follows Shakespeare's intended sequence. He seems to have planned two contrasting series: one about uncontrollable lust for a married woman of dark complexion (the "dark lady"), and one about conflicted love for a fair young man (the "fair youth"). It remains unclear if these figures represent real individuals, or if the authorial "I" who addresses them represents Shakespeare himself, though Wordsworth believed that with the sonnets "Shakespeare unlocked his heart".

"Shall I compare thee to a summer's day?

Thou art more lovely and more temperate ..."

—Lines from Shakespeare's Sonnet 18.

The 1609 edition was dedicated to a "Mr. W.H.", credited as "the only begetter" of the poems. It is not known whether this was written by Shakespeare himself or by the publisher, Thomas Thorpe, whose initials appear at the foot of the dedication page; nor is it known who Mr. W.H. was, despite numerous theories, or whether Shakespeare even authorised the publication. Critics praise the Sonnets as a profound meditation on the nature of love, sexual passion, procreation, death, and time.

Style

Shakespeare's first plays were written in the conventional style of the day. He wrote them in a stylised language that does not always spring naturally from the needs of the characters or the drama. The poetry depends on extended, sometimes elaborate metaphors and conceits, and the language is often rhetorical—written for actors to declaim rather than speak. The grand speeches in Titus Andronicus, in the view of some critics, often hold up the action, for example; and the verse in The Two Gentlemen of Verona has been described as stilted.

However, Shakespeare soon began to adapt the traditional styles to his own purposes. The opening soliloquy of Richard III has its roots in the self-declaration of Vice in medieval drama. At the same time, Richard's vivid self-awareness looks forward to the soliloquies of Shakespeare's mature plays. No single play marks a change from the traditional to the freer style. Shakespeare combined the two throughout his career, with Romeo and Juliet perhaps the best example of the mixing of the styles. By the time of Romeo and Juliet, Richard II, and A Midsummer Night's Dream in the mid-1590s, Shakespeare had begun to write a more natural poetry. He increasingly tuned his metaphors and images to the needs of the drama itself.

Shakespeare's standard poetic form was blank verse, composed in iambic pentameter. In practice, this meant that his verse was usually unrhymed and consisted of ten syllables to a line, spoken with a stress on every second syllable. The blank verse of his early plays is quite different from that of his later ones. It is often beautiful, but its sentences tend to start, pause, and finish at the end of lines, with the risk of monotony. Once Shakespeare mastered traditional blank verse, he began to interrupt and vary its flow. This technique releases the new power and flexibility of the poetry in plays such as Julius Caesar and Hamlet. Shakespeare uses it, for example, to convey the turmoil in Hamlet's mind:

> Sir, in my heart there was a kind of fighting
>
> That would not let me sleep. Methought I lay
>
> Worse than the mutines in the bilboes. Rashly—
>
> And prais'd be rashness for it—let us know
>
> Our indiscretion sometimes serves us well ...
>
> —Hamlet, Act 5, Scene 2, 4–8

After Hamlet, Shakespeare varied his poetic style further, particularly in the more emotional passages of the late tragedies. The literary critic A. C. Bradley described this style as "more concentrated, rapid, varied, and, in construction, less regular, not seldom twisted or elliptical". In the last phase of his career, Shakespeare adopted many techniques to achieve these effects. These included run-on lines, irregular pauses and stops, and extreme variations in sentence structure and length. In Macbeth, for example, the language darts from one unrelated metaphor or simile to another: "was the hope drunk/ Wherein you dressed yourself?" (1.7.35–38); "... pity, like a naked new-born babe/ Striding the blast, or heaven's cherubim, hors'd/ Upon the sightless couriers of the air ..." (1.7.21–25). The listener is challenged to complete the sense. The late romances, with their shifts in time and surprising turns of plot, inspired a last poetic style in which long and short sentences are set against one another, clauses are piled up, subject and object are reversed, and words are omitted, creating an effect of spontaneity.

Shakespeare combined poetic genius with a practical sense of the theatre. Like all playwrights of the time, he dramatised stories from sources such as Plutarch and Holinshed. He reshaped each plot to create several centres of interest and to show as many sides of a narrative to the audience as possible. This strength of design ensures that a Shakespeare play can survive translation, cutting and wide interpretation without loss to its core drama. As Shakespeare's mastery grew, he gave his characters clearer and more varied motivations and distinctive patterns of speech. He preserved aspects of his earlier style in the later plays, however. In Shakespeare's late romances, he deliberately returned to a more artificial style, which emphasised the illusion of theatre.

Influence

Shakespeare's work has made a lasting impression on later theatre and literature. In particular, he expanded the dramatic potential of characterisation, plot, language, and genre. Until Romeo and Juliet, for example, romance had not been viewed as a worthy topic for tragedy. Soliloquies had been used mainly to convey information about characters or events, but Shakespeare used them to explore characters' minds. His work heavily influenced later poetry. The Romantic poets attempted to revive Shakespearean verse drama, though with little success. Critic George Steiner described all English verse dramas from Coleridge to Tennyson as "feeble variations on Shakespearean themes."

Shakespeare influenced novelists such as Thomas Hardy, William Faulkner, and Charles Dickens. The American novelist Herman Melville's soliloquies owe much to Shakespeare; his Captain Ahab in Moby-Dick is a classic tragic hero, inspired by King Lear. Scholars have identified 20,000 pieces of music linked to Shakespeare's works. These include three operas by Giuseppe Verdi, Macbeth, Otello and Falstaff, whose critical standing compares with that of the source plays. Shakespeare has also inspired many painters, including the Romantics and the Pre-Raphaelites. The Swiss Romantic artist Henry Fuseli, a friend of William Blake, even translated Macbeth into German. The psychoanalyst Sigmund Freud drew on Shakespearean psychology, in particular, that of Hamlet, for his theories of human nature.

In Shakespeare's day, English grammar, spelling, and pronunciation were less standardised than they are now, and his use of language helped shape modern English. Samuel Johnson quoted him more often than any other author in his A Dictionary of the English Language, the first serious work of its type. Expressions such as "with bated breath" (Merchant of Venice) and "a foregone conclusion" (Othello) have found their way into everyday English speech.

Works

Classification of the plays

Shakespeare's works include the 36 plays printed in the First Folio of 1623, listed according to their folio classification as comedies, histories, and tragedies. Two plays not included in the First Folio, The Two Noble Kinsmen and Pericles, Prince of Tyre, are now accepted as part of the canon, with today's scholars agreeing that Shakespeare made major contributions to the writing of both. No Shakespearean poems were included in the First Folio.

In the late 19th century, Edward Dowden classified four of the late comedies as romances, and though many scholars prefer to call them tragicomedies, Dowden's term is often used. In 1896, Frederick S. Boas coined the term "problem plays" to describe four plays: All's Well That Ends Well, Measure for Measure, Troilus and Cressida, and Hamlet. "Dramas as singular in theme and temper cannot be strictly called comedies or tragedies", he wrote. "We may, therefore, borrow a convenient phrase from the theatre of today and class them together as Shakespeare's problem plays." The term, much debated and sometimes applied to other plays, remains in use, though Hamlet is definitively classed as a tragedy. (Source: Wikipedia)